THE CHANGING FACE OF CONSUMERISM

CHRISTOPHER NOSNIBOR

2013

Clinicality Press

York, England

THE CHANGING FACE OF CONSUMERISM

CHRISTOPHER NOSNIBOR

First published by Clinicality Press, York
http://clinicalitypress.com

ISBN 978-1-291-65037-2

The Changing Face of Consumerism

Introduction: the Changing Face of Blogging

Isn't it funny how things change? What's cutting edge one minute isn't only passé but horribly outdated and outmoded the next. One may argue that to an extent it was ever this, but in recent years, the pace of change seems to have accelerated almost exponentially. It isn't just me getting older: the facts speak for themselves. 50 or 60 years ago, few families had cars. Now, few families don't have cars, and no-one goes to school or market by horse and cart any more. CDs officially hit the mass market in 1983, but didn't really take off until near the end of the decade. The CD was supposed to revolutionise audio in every way. 'Tomorrow's World' declared the new discs 'indestructible' and 'the future', and while the former very soon proved to be an overstatement, they did bring about the demise of the audiocassette, and annihilated vinyl sales. And now? There are many buying – or obtaining – music who have never owned a physical copy of anything in their lives. Why would anyone want a CD that takes up all that *space*? Why would you buy a big, bulky stereo when you can have all the music you need on your phone?

Technology has played a major part in the unprecedented pace of change we're now witnessing, but there's more to it than that. Markets have changed. Consumers have changed. Culture has changed. And continues to do so.

Back in 2007, I set up a MySpace account with a view to promoting my writing. Everyone else was doing it, so it made sense to get in on the action. Social networking was hot, it was cool, it was now.

Bands were made on MySpace. They no longer needed a major label budget: they could build an audience direct.

Initially, I simply networked, connecting with people with common interests. Then I began blogging. The idea was to simply post excerpts of my fiction in the hope that people would latch on to it, start following my blog and buy by books. In hindsight this was an incredibly naïve approach, although creating an enigmatic mystique has worked for some. Maybe I'm just no good at being enigmatic. Moreover, it wasn't long before the urge to pass comment on things – books, music, life, the world around me. What began as a one-off rant about the demise of the record store following the news that my local record shop, where I had been going every Monday to purchase new releases on vinyl for a good number of years, was to close, became an occasional series. It was, as I saw it, a real-time commentary based on first-hand observations, made possible by the medium. That series forms the basis of this book.

As it was effectively written over the course of some five years, as a reaction to, reflection of, and response to rapidly occurring changes, so some of the first posts – reproduced here as the first chapters, may have dated somewhat already. In a sense, rather than rendering the book pointless, this is pivotal to the overarching idea of this book. The nature of consumerism is changing *fast*. So fast, in fact, that it's virtually impossible to keep abreast of progress. Nostalgia isn't what it used to be, and while previous generations may lament the loss of those things that defined bygone ages that were truly bygone ages, the pace of cultural change means society (broadly and generally speaking), is growing nostalgic for a past while it's still present. The 'outdated' chapters in this book, in the time I've spent working on the final chapters, have became

The Changing Face of Consumerism

historical, documents of a time when things were not necessarily simpler or even better, but different. Having existed as a consumer in the 80s and 90s – with changing needs and changing budgets – I've witnessed the changes of the last 20 years first-hand, and I don't believe for one moment that the preceding decades represent some 'golden age' of consumerism, and the changing face of consumerism has been both a positive and negative experience on a personal level. I reflect fondly on my years working in a second-hand record store in the 90s, although it's tempered with a sadness on account of the fact it couldn't happen now and there's an emerging generation (of real music fans, too) who don't even know what a record is, and are unlikely to even see a second-hand record store, let alone set foot in one as a shopper or worker.

The original chronology of the posts has been preserved primarily as a means of charting the rapid evolution I have made the key focus of the book's exploration. That said, not all of the pieces here have previously been published as blogs or otherwise, and there have been one or two minor edits and corrections made along the way. This doesn't detract from the idea that spurred me to compile these pieces. The simple fact remains: for better or worse, the times they are indeed a-changing, and this book provides a snapshot that charts but a brief but tumultuous period in consumer society, from the perspective of one man in a small corner of the UK. It represents his – my – opinions. I'm not an economist or sociologist (beyond an A-Level attained back in the 90s) and I make no pretence of representing a detailed, researched, academic-level critique. I'm just telling things as I see them.

Christopher Nosnibor

The Changing Face of Consumerism I: Vinyl Analysis

I love the Internet, I really do: have done for many years now. And I've long celebrated the widespread availability of, well, practically everything on-line. Essentially, if it exists, it can be found on the net. Where finding the *real* news, obtaining information on an infinitely broad range of subjects, tracking down that rare, obscure and out of print book title or record is concerned, it can't be beaten. It's a shop and a world-scale library accessible from the comfort of wherever you're comfortable. And it's also a brilliant way of meeting people: not only on MySpace, which has to be the greatest invention since the Internet itself (yes, even better than eBay), but elsewhere. Mrs Nosnibor will concur with me on this...

I also love music, as anyone who knows me personally, or has read my 'about me' section here on MySpace – or, better still, has read *Bad Houses* – will know. So yesterday I got up bright and early and headed down to my local record store: the new Shellac album was out, and having waited seven years since the last one, I was really quite excited by the the prospect of picking up their new slab of analogue noise on heavyweight vinyl. But on heading upstairs to the vinyl counter, I was informed that they hadn't got the new Shellac LP in yet. And nor would they be stocking it – or any other new releases for that matter. In fact, the shop wouldn't be stocking anything in another five or six weeks, because it will no longer be trading.

So what, you may ask, it's just another small shop closing, no big deal. It happens all the time. But that's just it: it *does* happen all the time.

The Changing Face of Consumerism

And herein lies the problem, the negative face of capitalism illustrated in the microcosm. The guy behind the counter said the shop's imminent closure was due to a shift in the market. "Nobody buys records anymore," he said. "The kids don't buy records anymore... students don't buy records anymore... people with young families don't buy records... and we're competing against the world." By 'records' he was also meaning CDs: sales have been dropping as downloads have become the most popular 'format.' He's right: nobody – apart from anal wax fans like myself and old bastards who've not kept abreast of technology – buys records anymore. But for those who do still buy records – and CDs – shopping on-line just isn't the same. The experience of rifling through racks of vinyl is unique and special. Finding the record you've been looking for, or finding a record that intrigues you and makes you want to buy it even though you'd not been looking for it and until a few moments ago didn't even know existed, is truly magical.

Don't get me wrong, I download stuff – but it's always tracks I'd not be seen dead buying anyway and so would have otherwise simply gone without, tracks I can't get anywhere else because they've been deleted for donkey's years and that I could only get second-hand anyway, or tracks by bands I'm curious about but don't want to fork out fifteen quid on their album to find out if they're any cop. If they are, I usually go out and buy the item anyway, so it's all good.

Until now, I've always argued that downloading wasn't going to really harm music: home taping *didn't* kill music, CDs didn't really kill off vinyl (although it was rather badly wounded for a while back there) and I didn't expect downloading to be any different. Apparently I was wrong.

Christopher Nosnibor

I first visited Track when I visited York at the age of 14 (I think). I officially began my record collection on said visit, purchasing The Sisters of Mercy's 'Reptile House EP,' 'Temple of Love' and 'Alice' on 12" plus 'Psychonaut' by Fields of the Nephilim, also on 12" that had been released the week before. Coming from a small backwater with only a tiny Overprice as a source of music, this was a revelation to me. I never thought then that I'd find myself a resident in York and that Track would become my local dealer. But it did, and I came to rely on it even more after the awesome Depth Charge closed. having been trading since the late 70s, it's been an important place for many record buyers like myself for a long time. Its closing will mark the end of an era. The choice of vinyl LPs and 7" singles in HMV is gash, and Virgin don't even stock vinyl. I can buy on-line, but it's not the same, and there are postage costs on top.

What about consumer choice? Arguably, it's consumer choice that's calling the death knell for the independents – not just record shops, but independent stores of all kinds. By going for the cheapest option, the MOR option, following the mainstream and buying what they're sold... fine, but by fuelling a move toward lowest-common-denominator consumerism, the choice is, in truth, rapidly diminishing.

I'm not going to say 'don't download' or 'don't shop in HMV' but for fuck's sake, if you have a local independent, use it... and let me know where it is, because I want my records to be records, and to buy them from someone who cares...

The Changing Face of Consumerism

The Changing Face of Consumerism II: Serious Fucking Racket

Well after some trouble with the Post Office – they tried to deliver while I was out, I requested redelivery via the website, they didn't redeliver so I waited in all Saturday morning for no reason and got up stupidly early on the Monday and walked all the way to the depot to collect it myself – I finally got my Shellac LP. Hoorah! Well, no, not quite. Despite appearing well packed, the record had managed to push a 2" split in one edge of the inner sleeve, and 5" split in the bottom of the inner sleeve... this split went right through the outer sleeve, too, so the vinyl was hanging out the bottom like a sagging buttock in a too-short mini-skirt. There was also a large dint in the outer sleeve, and a corresponding ruckle in the slip-cover. In short, it was fucked. So I've had to send it back – at a cost of £2.90 – and am now awaiting a replacement. *So what, things get damaged in the post all the time, desist in your whinging*, some of you are probably saying. But this wouldn't have happened if my local shop was still open. I'd have walked down on the day of release, bought the record – without the additional postage cost – and that would have been that. And all because the 'kids' are downloading music....

In the absence of the new Shellac LP, I've not been without new music. Fortunately, the new Whitehouse album, *Racket*, is a corker. Picking up where last year's *Asceticists* left off, this release sees Bennett & Best pursue a distinctly percussive avenue of sound. That's not to say they've gone conventional: the beats seem to be of Afro-Caribbean origin, and largely disorientatingly arrythmic, shuddering and irregular in the same way as the banging, grinding backings to tracks like 'Wriggle

Christopher Nosnibor

Like a Fucking Eel' are. Almost half of the album is instrumental, but the breaks are hardly cosy, and the quieter instrumental sections are dark and unsettling, and pave the way perfectly for the tracks when the vocals – as abrasive and relentless as ever – kick in. 'Dumping More Fucking Rubbish,' while treblier than its previous incarnation on *Asceticists*, is truly scary – by which I mean that it's exhilarating and Bennett's vocals are manic and nothing short of fucking brilliant. Certainly my album recommendation of the week.

The Changing Face of Consumerism

The Changing Face of Consumerism III: Forever Autumn

Some weeks ago, I began typing a piece that I intended to post as a blog. It was about the shift through Autumn, and how the visibly shortening days invariably put me in a strange place, how I become prone to moments of maudlin contemplation about how another year's passed and I've failed to achieve everything I sat out to by some self-imposed and ultimately meaningless deadline. I suppose in part it's because as the nights draw in and the leaves yield to leave bare skeletal frames, notions of life-cycles, and, consequently, the aging process and mortality are more visible, more tangible than at any other time of the year. Or perhaps that's just my perception. The piece I was working on was also going to touch on the stultifying effect of the encroaching darkness on my motivation, and, above all, my 'creativity.' But, perhaps somewhat ironically, I stalled on this piece, and a month on it's still not complete and seems ever so slightly inappropriate now: the moment has passed, and the flurry of snow I witnessed while making my first mug of Earl Grey this morning was enough to tell me we're in Winter proper now, not the Autumnal limbo I had been struggling to capture in words.

That isn't to say I lose the ability to write during the darker months. I can churn out as much through Autumn and Winter as during Spring and Autumn, it's just not always as easy to write using the same processes. But another reason this piece failed to come to fruition was because other projects became priority. One such project was the story 'Afterhours,' which Jim at Bad Marmalade has put out.[1] And as a brief

---

[1]   'Jim' is James Higgerson, who, after calling time on *Bad Marmalade* to pursue a PhD,

plug for someone who I think is making a concerted effort to get different stuff out there, I look forward to seeing the fully functional badmarmalade.com in the new year: it promises to be quite a multimedia extravaganza, and I'm all for multimedia extravaganzas. There's more besides, details of which I will divulge in due course.

But of course, as we reach the tail end of November, the fact that Christmas is looming is something that has become impossible to avoid. I've decided to be organised this year, and have already started my Christmas shopping. But whenever I'm out looking for gifts for other people, I find it difficult to refrain from rewarding myself, if not with actual purchases (as if I could afford to!), then by indulging myself with a flick round the book stored and record shops. And so it was a couple of evenings back I found myself in my local HMV. I suppose I should be pleased: there is no danger of me spending money I haven't got in light of their new marketing strategy, which seems to consist of filling the racks with DVD box sets and dozens of copies of 'key' CD titles at 2 for £10, 3 for £20 or whatever. And lo, HMV now resembles Fopp a couple of years ago. Before the chain collapsed. Yes, clearly it's a successful model. As such, my choice as a consumer has been eroded once more. I suspect that most people who want a copy of *Nevermind* have probably got one by now. And I suspect that anyone who buys one of the countless Westlife / Kylie / Coldplay (insert mass-consumption mainstream gash act here) CDs is a sucker who buys aural jissom they get pumped by Radio 1, etc. and is therefore entirely (albeit unknowingly) complicit with this corporate conspiracy.

---

went on to write the novel *The Almost Lizard*, published by Legend Press in 2013. Consequently, the 'multimedia extravaganza' version of *Bad Marmalade* never materialised.

The Changing Face of Consumerism

Anyone who has been with my bog for any time now may recall a series of rants about the closure of my local record store back in the summer. As a hardcore fan of vinyl, I was dismayed – to put it mildly – that the only independent record store in town – which also stocked every new release available on vinyl *on vinyl* – had been driven into liquidation by the market forces that always tend to reduce consumer choice rather than broaden it. But now things have become even more desperate: HMV no longer stocks *ANY* vinyl. And there's more: HMV (in York, anyway) no longer stocks singles. On any format. This is the same route that Zavvi (previously Virgin) took some time ago. Which means that now, not only can I not find the titles I want on vinyl, I can't even find the titles I want at all. Anywhere. And so once again I'm forced onto the Internet. Don't get me wrong: I like the Internet, but not for everything, and above all, I like choice.

But despite the best efforts of the music industry, the technology giants, the capitalist system at large (and, lest we forget, despite the fact that people are inherently lazy and allow themselves to be driven toward the easiest media to obtain), I shan't be changing my preferred medium and therefore shall not be switching to MP3. Not least of all because they're compressed to fuck and sound crap. Not least of all because even though it's becoming impossible to move in Nosnibor towers for records, I like getting not just the music, but the artwork and the physical object I've paid for. Not least of all because I don't want to think that just because my hard drive corrupts or my portable music player gets lost or stolen, I've lost my entire music collection.

And while we're on the subject of corporate giants and the Internet, I was rather tickled to discover this evening that *Bad Houses* is now listed on the Tesco website. In the fiction / literary category. Three down from Conan Doyle, and four above Jane Austen. Now, I hate Tesco and refuse to shop there, and so seeing my book being stocked (albeit virtually) is something I have mixed feelings about. They're even offering it at 5% lower than publisher's price. Which is good news for consumers I suppose...

The Changing Face of Consumerism

The Changing Face of Consumerism IV.III: X-Factor Christmas Number One Shocker (2009 edit)

'What goes around comes around' is a phrase I use often, although I find myself using it far more frequently in writing than in speech. Perhaps that's because I wrote more than I talk. Who knows? Anyway, as my last two blogs detailed, I'm quite acutely attuned to the cyclical nature of the seasons, and of life, and seasonal (mal)adjustments are an inevitable part of my biological and psychological calendars. To take a line from a song by Love Spit Love (Richard Butler is, in my opinion, one of the greatest – and possibly most underrated – lyricists to have emerged from the post-punk era), 'the only thing that's gonna stay the same is change.'

And so it is that this time last year I was complaining that 2008 had been a crap year in so many ways, not least of all culturally. The same is true of 2009. The recession continues, more shops are closing, job losses and crap culture mean 2009 has been very much like 2008, only shitter. This year there are no independent record shops to lose, so we're waving farewell to Borders and Threshers instead. And seeing as we're a month away from Christmas and the remaining shops are filling up with the same old tat and the television stations are hyping the same old films and the record labels churn out more of the usual fodder, it's perhaps fitting that I should revisit the blogs I posted a year ago, and also the year before. If nothing else, it saves me having to come up with anything new, and perfectly proves, by means of illustration, just how sickeningly tiresome such repetition is, and just how predictably what goes around comes around...

The 2008 introduction

I'm a pretty forward-thinking kind of guy. After all, it certainly pays to be forward thinking, and there's little to be gained by living, or wallowing, in the past. But having said that, I do find myself making frequent recourse to the past. There's a lot of it, and as such, there's really no escaping it and no point in denying it. And of course, we can learn a lot from the past, if we're so willing. Could many disasters, mishaps, accidents, wars and the current financial situation have been avoided if people had just looked back as well as forward? Quite possibly.

So, right now I'm like Janus, simultaneously casting my eye both back and forth. And all the while keeping an eye on the present: yes, the mystical third eye. So, in the present, we have yet another year of X-factor under way. No, I'm not watching it. It's simply nigh on impossible to completely avoid it. From the past, I happened upon a blog I posted late last December, entitled 'X-Factor Christmas Number One Shocker / The Changing Face of Consumerism IV.' I ran a number of occasional blogs in the 'changing face of consumerism' series, and it's something I may return to in 2009. Anyway, looking to the future, I realised that it was, conceivably, possible to predict what may come by drawing on my knowledge of past events. So this is no crystal-ball gazing, this is an education prediction. Let's see if I'm right in a couple of months time. It'll be a grim satisfaction if I am.

The Changing Face of Consumerism

X-Factor Christmas Number One Shocker / The Changing Face of Consumerism IV.II

I suppose it was inevitable really. Despite the efforts of [INSERT SOMEONE WHO THINKS THEY'RE CLEVER HERE] to outmanoeuvre the hype machine with some tongue-in-cheek alternative hype, there weren't really any other contenders for the supposedly coveted UK Christmas Number 1 slot. And so, for the third / fourth / fifth / sixth / etc (delete as appropriate) year in succession, the winner of X factor, the ITV 'talent' content that runs for what seems like about 50 weeks of the year, has had the best selling single at Christmas.

Congratulations to [INSERT NAME OF X-FACTOR WINNER HERE]. No, really: I don't have any real issues with him/her, other than that s/he was compelled to audition for such a credibility-free contest, and [INSERT NAME OF SOME SMUG GOBSHITE CELERITY] was backing him/her from the off (well s/he has to do something to keep themselves hip with the kids, right?). But I do have serious issues with the process.

I'm not saying that the whole audition / rehearsal / live performance / public voting / etc. process isn't hard work or nerve-wracking for contestants, but really, when it comes down to it, what we're watching is a glorified and overhyped karaoke competition. And the public fucking love it. They get to vote for their favourite, and the lucky winner, who's already done all of the necessary marketing and promotion for the last few months on prime-time television, gets to put out a record that half the nation are going to buy because they voted for it. Yes, the public gets what the public wants. And once again, the public wants mediocre slop. I can cope with that: it was ever thus. But what's the alternative?

Aye, there's the rub: there is no alternative, at least not that's readily available or easily accessible. And this is where I return to a point I've made on various occasions throughout the year on this (and other people's) blogs: the marketplace is becoming less competitive, not more. Consumer choice is practically a myth. While the large corporations (in all industries, not just music) are so fixated on finding the Next Big Thing – and fast – the idea of the next medium-sized thing and the slow-burning long-term investment thing ceases to be of interest. They want success and they want it NOW! The shareholders want to see a return – NOW – and in order to achieve these things, there's no scope for taking a gamble. If an executive makes one wrong decision, they're out of a job (although probably given a substantial golden handshake for their royal fuck-up because that's how it works these days. There are rewards for failure if you're high enough up the corporate ladder. But I digress...)

Readers may recall my bemoaning the closure of York's last independent record store a while back, and may also remember, more recently, my griping about the fact that neither of the remaining two stores, HMV and Zavvi (formerly Virgin) were stocking singles any more, on any format. Well, I dropped into HMV earlier this week to find that HMV were actually stocking singles again. That is to say, *a* single, and they had literally hundreds of it on special display stands around the store. Yup, [INSERT NAME OF X-FACTOR WINNER]'s single, [INSERT CORNY TITLE HERE]. At £3.99 a copy. Four fucking quid! So what if I wanted to buy a different single? Tough shit. If I wanted a single, it was '[INSERT CORNY TITLE HERE] or nowt. Suffice it to say I left with nowt.

The Changing Face of Consumerism

My local Sainsbury's is tiny and poorly stocked, but it's within reasonable walking distance (quite important for someone who doesn't drive). It doesn't really stock many CDs – a few greatest hits and various artists compilations and perhaps the top ten chart albums. Again, this doesn't exactly represent a great choice. But no matter. My local Sainsbury's doesn't stock singles. But wait, what's this? I strolled in yesterday evening for a few groceries and was stunned to see, by the entrance, a huge display stand of black cardboard with a huge red X on top. The plague? Yes and no: row upon row of , [INSERT NAME OF X-FACTOR WINNER] singles. At £3.99 apiece. Four fucking quid! Etc, etc.

Like CCTV springing up on every street corner, within a matter of days there's been a viral explosion of these CD displays. It's remarkable how quickly they've managed to record it, get the artwork done, the CD pressed and distributed. Anyone would think the record company had known all along. Makes one wonder just how much of the million-pound recording contract that is the X Factor prize goes into subliminal messaging during the series... especially amid the outcry from fans of [INSERT CONTENDER HERE] who said they couldn't get through (although I can't say that bothers me too much, because [INSERT CONTENDER HERE] is a cock anyway and we all know these things are rigged).

So what's my point? It's hard to say any more. I've never been lethargic in seeking out the things I like, however underground, esoteric or unobtainable via the more obvious commercial channels. But I'm growing increasingly frustrated by the evermore obvious squeeze being placed on choice. Most people won't go to the lengths I'm willing to, and the casual buyer simply won't purchase something they can't find. Put

Christopher Nosnibor

simply, artistic merit and even the idea of quality is being shunned in favour of a quick buck. I'm convinced it's not sustainable, but right now I can't see where it will end.

The Changing Face of Consumerism

The Changing Face of Consumerism V: Railing Against Transport Injustice

I could have posted this blog every year for the last decade and it would still have been relevant.

That rail passengers have been shafted over again is hardly news. Every year it's the same. And unsurprisingly, it's been widely reported as a source of indignation for travelers – mostly commuters, of course.

Now, I understand that operating costs aren't coming down: fuel might not be bargain basement right now despite costs coming down again, rail staff want paying decent salaries – for which I can't blame them – and everything they buy in, from repairs to toilet paper, isn't getting any cheaper on an annual basis. I can deal with that.

But what I can't deal with is the fact that most people who travel by rail do so because they either desperately want to leave their cars at home, for whatever reason, be it congestion, speed of transit or environmental reasons, all of which are valid reasons, many of which should be applauded, or simply because they cannot drive.

Now, I cannot drive, and I choose not to because a) I can't afford to b) I simply cannot drive: have never learned c) I don't see driving as a sound environmental choice. Now I'm not asking for a medal here, but if our government is as keen to go green as it claims, I should get something. Like access to a subsidised rail service, the likes of which they have in Japan, Australia and many parts of mainland Europe.

I particularly believe I – or the rail network – should get something now, not because of the economic situation per se – the news article suggests that rail prices should come down because the price of other goods are being lowered by companies in order to entice buyers – but because while our government is happy to chuck endless cash at banks who were too unscrupulous and greedy to lend sensibly, and at people who've been stupid enough to land themselves eyeball-deep in debt, all too often by buying 4-bedroom houses they couldn't afford simply to impress their friends, and at various failing car firms whose days are likely to be numbered anyway (cars are only going to be so useful when we've bled the oil reserves dry), there doesn't seem to be much on offer for the prudent, the sensible, the conscientious. Or the genuinely poor for that matter. Let's face it, a 2.5% cut in VAT only adds up to anything if you're spending heaps. What if you've not got heaps to spend – and therefore 'save' – in the first place?

Ordinarily, I'd say that consumers should vote with their wallets, and with their feet, by taking their custom elsewhere. But in this instance, such a protest simply doesn't work. What am I going to do? Say 'fuck you, I'll learn to drive and buy a car instead?' Er, hardly, given that even if I wanted to drive, I simply couldn't afford the lessons, and then to purchase and run a car. And besides, I don't make many journeys where to drive would be preferable to going by train. What's more, I can't very well read or whip out my notebook and start writing if I'm behind the wheel. So what other alternatives are there? 'Screw you, I'll stay at home and only travel within walking distance of my house unless you reduce fares?' Yeah, right. Ultimately, I'm afraid to say I can't see a solution.

The Changing Face of Consumerism

Prices are rising, but salaries aren't, and where they are, it's hardly in proportion to the escalating cost of living.

While in the commercially-orientated original version of this piece I suggested that cycling was the way forward, I fully appreciate that this is not a practical solution to the problem. Sure, for local journeys, it's a fine, virtually free and environmentally sound alternative to driving or busses and a lot faster than walking, but there's no way one could commute between cities on a daily or even weekly basis by bike. And I'm not about to cycle to Leeds and then pedal all the way home at half eleven at night after six pints, even if I thought I might be able to make it to work the following morning.

In short, it's not a matter of choice: like it or lump it, cause rail users are over a barrel.

Which leaves me in the position of being just one more dissatisfied consumer needing to let off steam and considering a trip to the bike shop.

The Changing Face of Consumerism VI: What's in a Name? Reinventing the Wheel to Create a Brand New Brand

Companies change their names all the time. It's not always a matter of choice: the Virgin Megastores had to lose the Virgin name once Richard Branson ejected them from his empire, although I'm sure they could have done better than Zavvi, which sounded for all the world like a low-grade takeaway pizza place, the kind favoured by students after a hard night's drinking. And although the company's demise not too long after the change was completely unrelated to the new moniker, I can't help but wonder how much good it did their sales.

Recent years have seen many companies adopt abbreviated versions of their original names, because they're snappier, and because they're the names by which most people referred to them in the first place. Hence, British Telecom became BT and Kentucky Fried Chicken became KFC (that they had to drop 'Chicken' from the name because it breached trade descriptions is, as far as I can find, an urban legend.

Other changes have come about as the result of mergers, something that's been occurring a lot in the banking sector in recent years. Again, that not all of these mergers have been entirely optional is rather by the by. And so The Midland Bank became part of the much larger Hong-Kong and Shanghai Banking Corporation, or HSBC (which makes the fact they refer to themselves as HSBC Bank here in England rather irksome). Halifax and Bank of Scotland merged to form HBOS. What will happen in the long term to this merged identity now they're a part of the Lloyds Banking Group remains to be seen. Abbey –formerly

The Changing Face of Consumerism

Abbey National – was recently acquired by Grupo Santander, the Spanish banking corporation, and along with a number of other companies, will soon be known simply as Santander. Well that simplifies things, and it's always good to know you're dealing directly with a global giant, rather than a global giant disguised as something smaller and more friendly.

On the subject of global giants, one company that has poured a lot of money into a name change – or 'rebrand' is Aviva, formerly Norwich Union in the UK and Aviva (amongst other things) elsewhere. Of course, the first step in choosing a new name (after the initial 'brainstorming' session where a bunch of overpaid marketing execs chuck ideas round for a few hours before drawing up a shortlist of the least corny or ridiculous) is basic research. And I mean basic. Double-check the meanings of the names you've got in the dictionary. Google it. Chances are, if you've had an idea, someone else has already had it, especially if it's any good. So it's no good, if you run a taxi firm, going with the intention of calling it A2B, and then being amazed that there's already an A2B in the area. It's the very least you should do before sinking a reputed £80M into an advertising campaign and all the other things like systems and stationery changes required for such a gargantuan identity overhaul. It's a lesson hard-learned by the former polytechnic in Newcastle, which began work on a rebrand to the City University of Newcastle upon Tyne before someone spotted the potentially problematic acronym.

According to their press, Aviva was chosen for its apparent lack of obvious connotations, and for sounding bright and zesty. They also note that it is a Hebrew name which means Spring or Renewal. So, sort of appropriate to the idea of a rebrand being a rebirth, one could say, but hardly without association. Not being a particularly Jewish company, it doesn't seem entirely appropriate. A recent survey suggested that the majority of people in the UK think it's a type of car. It's hard to deny that it is quite similar to the Vauxhall Viva. And while it may also sound rather similar to Arriva ('one of the largest transport services organisations in Europe, employing some 34000 people and delivering more than one billion passenger journeys across 12 European countries ever year'), at least it's original, right?

Well, at the time Norwich Union settled on their future name, there was Aviva Cosmetic Dentistry in Hertfordshire, Aviva: women's world-wide web, a 'free, international, feminist webzine,' Aviva Natural Cleaning Products, the Aviva School of Midwifery, and the Aviva High School 'for girls in need of special education,' to name but a few, all operating and appearing on major search engines. And what of the manufacturers of the Accu-Chek Aviva Glucose Meter? Obviously, it's impossible to predict, but perhaps the lesson to be learned from this – apart from that the adage 'look before you leap' is one that has considerable merit and that planning really is everything – is that size isn't everything, and money can't buy you anything, least of all uniqueness.

The Changing Face of Consumerism

The Changing Face of Consumerism VII – and Zavvi Comes Good

Having spent much time in recent months beefing about the increasing difficulty I have in obtaining vinyl records, even new releases, and how this is symptomatic of a broader cultural shift in the consumerist society, it's as unexpected as it is nice to be able to say something positive for a change.

I've always been an advocate of the independents, and of the chains preferred HMV. Virgin, now Zavvi, was always more expensive and carries a comparatively limited, mainstream-orientated range. But recently, when HMV in York stopped carrying vinyl – or even singles – the difference became less significant. So, arriving in Sheffield and strolling downstairs in Zavvi (the music's been demoted to the basement, out of sight, in favour of the games and DVDs that are what really entice the punters into what's supposed to be a *music* store) – somewhere to go to avoid the inclement conditions – I was elated to find... vinyl! A 7" rack! And, in relative terms, a huge rack (heh heh) of vinyl LPs! Ok, so a lot of mainstream pap and a lot of neo-indie (i.e. indie by style / genre, not by virtue of being on an independent label) pap, but some good shit too, including Ministry's *The Land of rape and Honey*, Nirvana's *Bleach* reissued on clear vinyl, 3 volumes of The Upsetter complete singles box set series, and *Year Zero* by Nine inch Nails, which I wasn't even aware had received a vinyl release. All were chronically overpriced, but I felt obliged to buy at least *something*, if only to prove that the demand for vinyl exists. And *year Zero* is pressed on two particularly hefty chunks of wax, and is very nicely packaged...

On leaving the store, I couldn't help feeling I'd been rather extorted, and that I had been compliant in my own extortion in my vague notion of supporting some kind of consumer revolution or backlash. Who was the loser here? But then I wondered if the price I'd paid was really so expensive? I'd not had to pay postage on an item that would arrive battered, beaten and bent having been sat on and used as a frisbee for a week or more, so on balance...

I can't pretend I've changed my mind about the state of the market or that I'm optimistic about the future, but for today, at least, I'm rather cheered.

The Changing Face of Consumerism

The Changing Face of Consumerism VIII: Made-up Nonsense for Sale: Sci-Fusion, the New Trend in Advertising

Advertisers have long – if not always – relied on the gullibility of the consumer. It must work, too, otherwise no companies would bother to pay hundreds of thousands, even millions of pounds on advertising campaigns. I've even found myself affected by the power of suggestion, thinking that I might like pizza for tea after an ad for Pizza Hut or something. And, while it's rare that I will actually make a purchase based on an advertisement, adverts have had a deep effect on my life, and being something of a cultural sponge, I can still recall countless ads from the 80s ver batim, including those for obscure and long-discontinued products (not so much a simple case of the bounty hunters are here, they're searching for paradise or wooooooahhhh, Bodyform, as don't you wish you had a Mitsubishi, or they're so good, they're Good 'n' Crunchy crisps, anyone?).

Back in the old days, when advertising was unsophisticated and consumer needs were a lot more simple, it was enough to simply show a picture of the product and say what it did, or perhaps how good it was – even if it meant lying. So, for example, slogans (straplines didn't exist then) such as 'Bile Beans – keep you healthy, bright-eyed and slim' did the trick. Other classics include 'Guinness is good for you!' 'Eat Lard' 'Craven A: smooth on the throat' 'Smoking – good for your health and your image' etc.

In recent years, advertising standards have taken all the fun out of advertising. It's no longer permissible to lie or misrepresent a product for starters. To sidestep this sort of legislation, advertisers began to blind target markets with science and statistics. This has reached a new level of absurdity recently: claims regarding popularity are substantiated with survey response figures tucked at the bottom of the screen – even if the surveys were bollocks and represent nothing. '80% of women agree that our skin cream is the best skin cream under a fiver they've ever used'* *sample of 9 women, July 2009.

It's no longer acceptable to be sexist or racist in adverts any more, either, unless it's against men (never mind the man as sex-object cliché, which grew tired before we'd all finished our 'Diet Coke break,' I've seen several products that are, apparently, so simple that even a man could use them. Oh, that's so ironic and postmodern!)

The current vogue in advertising is an extension of 'the science bit,' with ads pushing to demonstrate scientific innovation, in which advertisers shout about the fact that the product you're being sold is revolutionary! It runs something like this: 'We've come up with a new formula... it's so new and different from anything else we've had to make up a nonsensical name for it, that's based on a pseudoscientific corruption of what it's supposed to do.' There's a formula for describing the formula, too: take either a noun or verb that describes what the product is or does, and meld it to an adjective that describes in an appealing or exciting way, how it does this.

I think I first noticed this form of sciadvertising when I switched to Acuvue one a day contact-lenses. I could immediately see more clearly: I suppose you could say that with my sharper vision, my my view was more accurate. Adjectinouns and verbectives are now rife. And why not? They're perfect for encapsulating the entire essence of a product.

The Changing Face of Consumerism

Take, for example, a toothpaste that locks in minerals to preserve the enamel. 'A toothpaste that locks in minerals to preserve the enamel' is too dry and too long-winded. But the unique 'enamelock' formula is something special, not to mention snappy-sounding. There are other toothpastes on the market that also boast great ways of preventing your breath from smelling like shit and shifting unsightly plaque, too. Aquafresh has rare oxygen-based isotopes in the mix as its active ingredient, and the frothing that shifts the gunk from the gums isn't just a froth of oxygen bubbles. No, that foam is the toothpaste's 'iso-active' element working.

There are more, many more, great scientific innovations on the market. What about an 'follow-on' milk for toddlers with ingredients that boost and fortify the child's immune system? That would be the immuno-fortis, then. Want a washing gel that contains oxygen that activates in the wash and actively lifts stains? Get the one with Actilift! And if you don't fancy gel or powder, why not use Liquitabs? Yes, they're tablets... with liquid in, geddit? Nasty verruca? Get Bazooka, it's got verrukill technology! Rough skin you feel the need to exfoliate with a brush? It's nothing to be ashamed of, and it's the reason Garnier have designed their special exfo-brusher. Or maybe it's Maybelline...

I've grown accustomed to pro-biotic yoghurts now. Everything seems to be pro-something in the advertising world, and I like those good bacteria that are in favour of my digestion. I'm a little unsure about those pre-biotic compounds though: if I want food that's already been digested, I'll got to McDonald's (do-do-do-do-do, it's full of shit).

We are, of course, supposed to be impressed. C'mon people, get a grip! These charlatans are selling the same crap tarted up and rebranded in fancy new packaging, but it's a pretty thin disguise. The new formula with its fancy pseudoscientific name is just made-up nonsense that's not an improvement created with the consumer in mind (unless you count the advertising execs in their sharp suits in the boardroom pondering how to fleece more cash from those they've already been fleecing blind for years, while increasing that number threefold in quarter one, etc). The reason I'm not buying is because this new mode of selling the same junk is an insult to our intelligence – that presents itself as appealing to our intelligence by presenting dumbed-down pseudoscience as somehow sincere and actually scientific. The truth is, it's even worse than the 'universe centres around you, be selfish' pitches that tell the consumer, 'you're worth it' and 'it's all about you' etc. I say, wise up, don't buy this rehashed garbage and buy what you want or need, not what your sold. The feeling you'll get from doing so is grrrrrrrrrrrreat!

The Changing Face of Consumerism

The Changing Face of Consumerism IX: State of Independence, or, All's Well at The Inkwell

The seven 'Changing Face of Consumerism' articles I ran on MySpace in 2008 and 2009 all shared a common theme, namely lamenting the sad decline of the real – both in media and commodity, with 'reality' television being a pisspoor ersatz approximation of any reality I've ever known, and 'real' shopping experiences being slowly subsumed by the virtual marketplace.

Don't get me wrong, I'm all for progress, and have long been a big fan of on-line shopping, being one who doesn't cope well with crowds or endless hours of pavement-pounding in search of goods, but by the same token, I'm a strong advocate of consumer choice. Despite what the global marketplace on-line tells us, we as consumers do not have infinite choice, not least of all because while some niche outlets fare well on-line, many have gone to the wall because the same kind of corporate giants that slowly erased all of the small independent stores from the high streets of each and every town have steamrollered the little on-line traders out.

As city centres everywhere become identikit clones of anywheresville, so our sense of location becomes diminished: the only thing to differentiate, say, Leeds from Lincoln, isn't the choice of shops, but the size of each branch, and after a mooch round M&S, Boots, Game and HMV, stopping for a uniform coffee in a Starbucks or Costa before going on to... well, it doesn't matter. I mean it really doesn't matter where you are, the experience is pretty much the same. Fine, so you know what you're going to get, but the experience of discovering a little specialist shop tucked away somewhere is radically different and appeals to a whole range of senses. However hard Amazon try to replicate the browsing experience of specialist independent book and record stores with features like 'look inside' and the song snippets you can listen to, in addition to the list of recommendations based on what you're looking at and what other shoppers have also purchased or viewed that functions as a mimesis of the friendly and enthusiastic guy behind the counter who just loves his books or music and knows everything there is to know, like a living, walking encyclopedia, it just isn't the same. There's no substitute for browsing.

And so it was that I was practically skipping when The Inkwell opened in York a few weeks ago. A little shop stocking secondhand books, records (with a few selected new titles), CDs and cards, it's the kind of shop you used to drop into, rummage around and find something wonderful you didn't even know you wanted. The owner, Paul Lowman, is clearly an unashamed enthusiast first and a businessman second, and while such a venture is the kind that will never make him rich, and would make many lenders and entrepreneurs alike squirm in discomfort, it's a shopper's delight. Perhaps not surprisingly, The Inkwell is aimed at a niche market (by which I mean discerning shoppers: Paul's philosophy is according to the website, "COOL STUFF FOR ALL!" Popular Culture is about democracy – inclusivity, not exclusivity) specialising as it does in books on music, film and pop culture, with sections on the Beat Generation, Art, Philosophy and a noteworthy – not to mention impressive – selection of pulp paperbacks,

The Changing Face of Consumerism

all in remarkably good condition (yet reasonably priced, with titles marked up at between six and ten quid).

The vinyl, too, is all in great nick, and the range, though limited, is all about quality and catering to a particular kind of discerning alt/hipster customer. There's no mainstream pap to be found on the racks: instead, there are sections devoted to Garage, Psych, 90s Indie, Spoken Word / Comedy, and even Burlesque. Yes, if you want the kitsch sleaze of yesteryear, then the range of sexploitation titles in both audio and written media is exceptional.

It's a tiny little place, made all the more cramped by there being a pair of school desks in the middle of the room, upon which a choice of books are casually laid. It's all about the browsing experience (they serve coffee too), and an eclectic mix of music is spun – at high volume, and all on vinyl, naturally – on the turntable in the corner by the counter. Of course, it's simply one's man's vision, one man's obsession made manifest... but what's wrong with that? But equally, why should a shop such as this succeed in a climate where major chains are going to the wall? The answer, I believe, is simple. In attempting to appeal to everyone, the major chains ultimately cater for no-one. In aiming to cover a vast market based on some kind of assumed generic average consumer and broad populism, the chains become Xerox copies of one another: reliable, perhaps, but ultimately forgettable and wholly impersonal. A shop like The Inkwell isn't about conquering the world or trying to cater to all tastes: it knows its market and knows it well – because by being the shop its owner wants it to be, it's catering for like-minded individuals (there's that word again!). It's unique in every way, and every item in stock is essentially a one-off. It has the personal touch

37

and is memorable. And that's why it has a better than average chance of success.

So, on the opening day I left with a brand new hardback copy of *Brion Gysin: Dream Machine* (a bargain at a tenner given that it retails at £25), a read but respectable copy of *The Dark Stuff* by Nick Kent (£3) and a vinyl LP – a copy of *Fade Out* by Loop, again in top condition (EX as *Record Collector* would have it), for a fiver.

I returned this week and was pleased to see some of the stock had gone and new stuff had taken its place, meaning I was able to add a copy of the original 1971 Olympia Press edition of *S.C.U.M. Manifesto* by Valerie Solanas to my library. The tenner asking price was more than fair, especially given the condition.

Does The Inkwell represent the vanguard of the counter-revolution in the world of retail? Perhaps not, but I'd like to think that other independent stores will begin to pop up, not just in York, but in every city, and soon. It's unlikely that this is how the economic situation will be recovered, but being able to rifle some good books and records in a pleasant environment certainly makes these dark times a lot more bearable.

The Changing Face of Consumerism

The Changing Face of Consumerism X: The 'News' Smokescreen / Television: the Opium of the People

There's a very good chance that I've blogged and made comments on other blogs about the vapid, vacuousness of most television. There's an equally considerable chance I've remarked on what I consider to be the 'dumbing down' of the news media, the diminishing quality and standard of journalism and the lack of depth of news coverage. However, this last week has served to remind me, in bold neon graphics with a portentous theme tune punctuated with orchestral strikes, just how bad things have become.

After BBC's 'Breakfast' became a lifestyle show with a few brief news headlines thrown in, I switched to Sky News in the mornings, not because I thought it was great quality news coverage, but because it did at least provide news coverage, as well as weather forecasts and the like when advertised. The trouble is, Sky News now looks like 'Brasseye', only without the levels of literacy or the sense of its own absurdity.

I can accept the difficulties a 'slow news day' presents the producers and all involved, not least of all the journalists. However, I can't buy that there's ever a time when there is only one story worthy or reporting taking place in the entire world. To take a couple of recent examples, Raoul Moat's stand-off against the police and the rescue of the Chilean miners both received blanket rolling coverage on the UK's 24-hour news channels. Culminating in the fugitive murderer's suicide, the former was less 'news at it unfolded' and more live action televisual voyeurism. Did we actually need to see very little, shot in night vision, for several hours on end? What did the presence of continuous footage as it happened, accompanied by endless fill and speculation from the on-scene reporter actually give the viewers? Or more to the point, what did it give them that they needed?

The miners' rescue took on an almost gameshow-like quality as both Sky and the BBC added a counter on screen, the points clocking up each time another miner popped above ground. All done in real-time of course, with endless repetitive, empty commentary and replays of the previous men as they emerged from the collapsed mine, even making use of split screen to allow for re-runs from an hour before without having to miss a second of the drama as it unfolded in real time. The miners were repeatedly hailed as 'heroes,' naturally, although as one miner from another dangerous mine in Chile said, it's not heroism, but doing a job to put food on the table. Still, from the comfort of our centrally heated homes munching on hot toast with scrambled eggs before driving off to a comfortable air-conditioned office, most things that require physical labour and risk probably appear heroic. The context is all.

Fast forward a few days, and it's a slow news day. So the Chilean president's visit to England, bearing gifts of pieces of rock for the Queen is the main headline and speculation over funding cuts the government may or may not be about to announce occupy the majority of airtime. So, to compensate the lack of stories, Sky News ran an article on a Guinness World Record breaking chocolate bar. With the headlines on a fifteen-minute cycle, it soon became tedious. One of the newsreaders commented to another that the producers were asking her to drop the article, but that she thought it was important.

The Changing Face of Consumerism

It matters not whose decision it was. The point is, the news has long been full of these fluffy fillers, but now, alongside celebrity 'news,' such trivia seems to be slowly shunting the serious news aside in terms of coverage. Moreover, while giving space to pointless non-news, and providing disproportionately lengthy coverage which is startling lacking in substance to other stories, the question is 'where is the other news?'

What are they not telling us? TV news – as well as Internet news and most popular newspapers – is all about the headlines. There's the occasional 'expert' providing some soundbite opinion, and this is intended to give weight to the story. Most viewers and readers probably accept it at face value, but that's really all there is to accept: it's all about surface, appearance. A thirty-second interview with an 'expert' with dubious credentials is not the same as detailed analysis. How often is there any background or context given to a news event? How often are the real implications of a news item, such discussed? I'm not talking about the headline 'statistics', like the suggestion that if the limit on the tuition fees British universities can charge is removed, then tuition fees could soar to 'up to £12,000 a year' and 'the average student will graduate with £30,000 of debt', either. Precisely how are these figures calculated?

This last week, the burying of the real news with trivia and tabloid tittle-tattle was illustrated even more sharply by the blanket coverage and speculation over Wayne Rooney's decision to leave Manchester United. While everyone (and I mean everyone – the office was buzzing solidly for days over the story) worked themselves into a lather over this 'gobsmacking' turn of events, the government slipped out an emergency budget that will shaft the entire nation for decades to come. Half a million jobs are to go, and yet all the attention is on some whore-fucking Neanderthal who earns in a week more than many will earn in twenty years? Something is seriously wrong. Of course, I'm not suggesting that the timing of the two events was in any way planned or co-ordinated, but....

The dissemination of news is a fine balancing act. Too much bad news or detail and most viewers will turn off, declaring the coverage 'boring.' And in the current climate, it's all about ratings. Ratings (indirectly) bring revenue. So it's important to have mass appeal, and that means the tabloid-readers are as much the target audience as the serious broadsheet readers and business-types – if not more so. The business types are too busy working, welded to their Blackberry to watch television, and when they do have time, they want the headlines, fast. Every fifteen minutes, in fact. Not every hour, having to wait for analysis and waffle. But this need for swift, readily-digestible bitesize chunks comes at the expense of both depth and range.

So, for the perfect news programming, here's the strategy. Heap on the stories that will evoke panic and outrage: scare the viewers, and anger them enough to grumble to their friends and work colleagues (but not so much that they'll actually do anything: we don't want a world in which everyone downs tools and takes to the streets every time they're a bit disgruntled, like in France), while countering them with stories of what the government is doing for them to make their lives better or safer. That way, they'll stay in line and remain fearful while chuntering but not acting or protesting. Toss in just enough trivia to entertain and prevent the viewers from becoming completely depressed, and so after a grouse about this that and the other, they'll be able to chat about the cute

The Changing Face of Consumerism

animal story and then move onto the last night's soaps. The status quo is maintained, and life goes on while the world spirals deeper into chaos, recession and carnage.

Christopher Nosnibor

The Changing Face of Consumerism XI: Self-Publication is Not Vanity: Literature and the Punk Ethic in the 21st Century

What is the difference between self-publishing and vanity publishing? is there a difference? If so, what does it matter? The issues surrounding self-publishing and vanity publishing are divisive. Here's why self-publishing is a good thing.

As someone who writes (does that make a writer? Perhaps) and is always on the lookout for outlets for my work in this increasingly difficult market I subscribe to a service that emails me with details of any new publishers, agents, magazines, etc. over the last year, it's proven quite handy. I've tried my stuff with a few of the various zines listed, and even had a few successes. Occasionally, they also send me a newsletter, which contains, amongst other things, articles penned for authors, by authors. I tend to ignore these, in the main. It's not that I'm unwilling to take advice – I need all the advice I can get, to be honest – it's just that I feel that much of the advice is cack. I'm awkward like that: I also maintain that 'creative writing' is something that can't be taught, and have spent my career to date doing the precise opposite of what I've read in the countless essays and articles on how to write that I've happened upon. Apparently, to write successfully, you need a good, tight plot and believable characters that develop as your book progresses. But since none of the books I like to read follow these rules and I figure I'd rather produce works that I would want to read, I'd rather consign myself to 'failure' than follow the established formula.

The Changing Face of Consumerism

Anyway, one recent newsletter had as its lead an article by Malcolm Stewart, author of 'High Spirits,' entitled 'Self Publication is Vanity.' The title intrigued me – as did the subject, as an author who has self-published in the past, and intends to continue to do so – and so I read on.

Stewart writes that, 'vanity is the correct word, let us not dress it up. If you have to get published that way, you can probably afford it and it is good for your ego.' He goes on: 'There is a very strong urge to get your work published and out there, but I am sorry your vanity is just a useful tool for publishers to beat you with. '

Being a blog, it's all about the opinion, and Mr Stewart concludes not only with an opinion borne out of his own wealth of experience, but also dispenses some wonderful idealistic advice – because he can. He's been there, and so is qualified: 'I think everybody should just keep on going, until someone decides to publish you. Most of us know whether or not the book which we are trying to publish, is worth it. Although I am positive I would have carried on, even if I had thought my own book was rubbish. Although I never once considered paying someone to publish my book, if they didn't like it enough to have it published for commercial gain.'

For the time being, we should overlook the poor standard of prose and the not-quite-sentences beginning successively with 'although' and concentrate on the window over the dressing. From the outset it's clear that Malcolm considers self and vanity publishing to be one and the same. Historically, this may have been the case, but with the advent of PoD technologies and companies like Lulu, the whole nature of publishing is changing. No longer does having one's book published require substantial funds. Had there been a need to invest, well, anything, in order to put my own pamphlets out, I simply wouldn't have done it, as I do not possess the financial resources. Mr Malcolm also makes a number of other unfounded and iffy assumptions, not least of all in his assertion that if a writer can't get published it's because they simply aren't good enough. I myself have investigated the books of a number of major-league authors, only to be shocked and appalled by the abysmal quality of the prose (and Stewart's beginning two consecutive sentenced with 'although,' in a passage where he blatantly contradicts himself in stating that he wouldn't take his own advice to give up on a book makes me question his literary skills also). Moreover, Malcolm's equation of books that have commercial potential with quality is entirely erroneous. Since when did commercial success equal quality? And what has 'art' (under which broad umbrella literature falls) got to do with profit? Art has a long history of existing beyond the parameters of populism, and generally only enters the arena of popular culture once it has been diluted and repackaged. Self-publishing thus dispenses with the need to pander to whatever the publishing houses want to peddle to the punters (most are currently only interested in crime fiction, memoirs and teen vampires) and allows for literature that has more niche appeal to be placed in the public domain.

Bettie Corbin Tucker is more precise in her distinction between vanity and self-publishing. But then, she's an expert, and has written a book about it, and is ken to share her vast knowledge – at a price. In an article entitled 'What is POD Publishing? Should I consider it?' she writes:

The Changing Face of Consumerism

If you pay money to a publisher who publishes books using offset printing, they are a vanity or subsidy press. If you pay the money directly to a printer and bypass the publisher, you are self-publishing. Self-publishing is far more respected by the book industry. Vanity /subsidy publishers are known by reviewers, and your book usually won't get reviewed by the well-known reviewers. By the way, if you plan to self-publish the traditional way, think about purchasing my book on the subject. It is entitled *How To Self-Publish Your Book With Little or No Money* and is available on Amazon.com.

Now, I'll concede, there's good and bad to be found in this new era of zero-budget self-publishing opportunities. One big positive is the fact that publishing is no longer simply for the wealthy. And why should it be? Wealth has never been an indicator of taste or artistic ability, and good education doesn't a good writer make. I'm all for egalitarianism. What's more, whereas traditional publishing – vanity or otherwise – was reliant on distribution for the product to reach any potential market or audience, it is now possible have one's product available to a global audience on day of release. And in a world of shrinking markets, having the ability to reach a global market without the need for any kind of outlay means that the potential to reach an audience, while no means easy with everything that's flying around out there, is at least possible.

Of course, the flipside of egalitarianism is that anyone can do it, and the common criticism of self-publishing is that there's no quality control does indeed have a degree of merit. But the same is true of the Internet as a whole, and is true of music. Shit bands – I mean truly shit, can't sing, can't play a note, can't keep time bands – won't get many gigs, won't win many fans and won't sell many records or CDs, irrespective of who presses and sells them – be it a record label, the bandmembers' parents who think they're brilliant, or the band themselves. Yes, the public are stupid and have an unquenchable thirst for crap if it's marketed in the right way, but there are limits and they won't part with cash for complete tat all the time, even if the continued success of X-Factor finalists may suggest to the contrary.

However, the argument in favour of the 'quality control' the conventional publishing process supposedly ensures is also deeply flawed, on a number of levels. First, there's the fact that croneyism is endemic in the publishing industry – just as it is in so many other industries. Privilege breeds privilege and it's all too often the case that who you know counts for considerably more than what you know, what you've written, etc., etc.. In short, it's easy to bypass – or perhaps that should be buy-pass – the arduous slog and leapfrog over the struggling authors if your uncle John goes to the right golf club or whatever. This argument similarly assumes that editors are themselves literate and possess 'great taste' – whatever that may be.

In the music industry, artists are increasingly working to a DIY model, self-producing CDs and selling them at gigs and on-line. They're applauded for their 'punk ethic.' Besides, it's broadly agreed that the music industry is screwed, and that bands are probably better off going this route: it's harder to get shafted over if there's no-one holding the purse (and the rights to all of your recordings). Yet in the literary world, this approach is sneered at. It's this kind of snobbery that perpetuates the myth that self-publication is a bad idea, and is simply an exercise in

The Changing Face of Consumerism

vanity. Far from it: self-publishing represents the new literary underground, but with the added bonus that a writer has the potential to tap into a global readership. Small wonder the publishers, and those who believe in the power invested in publishers, don't like it.

In my personal experience, the most exciting writing to have emerged over the course of the last five years to so have been circulated by blogs, and through on-line magazines, and through tiny publishers, most of whom use PoD publishing.

And what of the mode of dissemination? Much has been made of the death of the book as the e-book gains popularity. But does anyone actually know anyone who owns an I-reader or other portable digital text reading device? I for one do not. Perhaps I move in the wrong circles. Perhaps I simply don't know many people sufficiently affluent. But I do know a lot of most avid readers, and they are all very much fans of real books. Yet amongst them, there are many who agree that much of the most exciting literature is to be found on-line. There is a consensus that publishers are too staid, too unwilling to take risks, and those that are lack the finance to really put challenging and innovative texts out because the challenges posed by the issues of marketing a difficult, genre-defying book. As such, both authors and readers alike are presented with something of a dichotomy. Readers prefer conventional books but those that seek unconventional text are compelled to do so on-line. Many authors are also readers – and so they ought to be – and yarn to see their works in print and to reach a mass audience, but are compelled to self-publish and put their work out on-line because it's not so much the most appropriate medium, but the *only* medium. This has been true in Hitchin's case. Although he recently published his first chapbook, *The Holy Hermaphrodite*, the route has been a very 21st century one. As he explained, 'The internet has allowed me to communicate with people and to publish work. Prior to becoming active on-line, I had no readership and only one publishing credit.'[2] He also states that 'The internet is necessarily fragmented; the average user sees/reads more than s/he intends to. This could be headlines, flashes of text, image, advertising... There is something absurd about publishing cut-ups on-line, as there is in posting independent literature on networking sites owned by huge commercial enterprises. I enjoy doing both.'[3]

We are often told that the Internet is the cutting edge, that the Internet is responsible for the death of the music industry, and that it will be responsible for the death of the publishing industry. To an extent, this may be true. It may be equally true that these industries which have for so long had a stranglehold on the arts are simply committing commercial suicide and bringing about their own demise.

I would suggest that it was inevitable. If, as Fredric Jameson suggests, postmodern fiction is borne out of postmodern culture and 'the logic of late capitalism' then the extreme fragmentation of culture and the emergence of sub-sub-subcultures (albeit as a reaction against or response to a homogenised global mainstream) which are driven as much by market forces as by any kind of artistic ideals will give rise to new problems of connecting with markets, even in the so-called 'global village' Marshall McLuhan wrote of. At this point, sustainability becomes an issue. People do seem largely unwilling to pay for art in any media if it

---

2   Hitchin, interview contained in *The Holy Hermaphrodite*

3   Ibid

can be obtained on-line, and it is consequently more difficult to make money from art, from music, from writing. And we are in uncharted waters: there are no models to draw on that offer the answers to these questions. I would contend that insofar as the cut-up works of Hitchin and Kenji Siratori are concerned, the medium and the message are indeed inextricably linked, a point on which Hitchin concurs.[4]

Given the closed nature of the publishing industry, and the absolute refusal of most publishers to take even the lightest risk, self-publishing is the way forward, the future of literature. And at this point, self-publishing is a matter of life or death, and vanity simply doesn't enter the equation.

---

[4]   Hitchin, interview contained in *The Holy Hermaphrodite*

Christopher Nosnibor

The Changing Face of Consumerism XII: Get a Little Bit Closer - Memoir, Accessibility and Brushing Virtual Shoulders with Celebrity

This is something that's seemingly crept up on me while I've been immersed in various writing projects and pouring over lyric books and websites while researching a story of indeterminate length I'm currently working on (just in case anyone thought I may have been dwelling in a cultural vacuum with no access to television or internet with my eyes closed and my fingers in my ears), because until recently I was largely unaware of the popularity of memoir and, equally, the accessibilising (yes, I'm coining a new term) of celebrities. Perhaps that's simply because although I like to think I have a reasonable idea of what's going on in the mainstream, I nevertheless tend to focus my energies on things that interest me. Really, life's too short to squander too much time on bad books, bad music, crap blockbusters and even crapper television programmes. Which means that while I will drop in on Big Brother every now and again, I'm not wired to the box 24/7 for the 3 months or whatever it's on for.

Now, I already knew that biographies (and crummy autobiographies ghosted for retard pseudo-celebrities who've done precisely fuck all in their short overprivileged lives) have topped the best seller lists for some years now, and that the proliferation of bollocks magazines like OK! Grazia, etc., etc., ad nauseam, all filled with grainy paparazzi shots of sagging tits and bad cellulite is more than evidence of our obsession with 'celebrity' and also with propagating the all-too-obvious fact that all that separates these figures of international renown is, in essence, a bank balance and a publicist. Yes, your favourite celebrity, for all their fame and wealth, has a spare tyre just like you, gets pissed and looks like crap at 2 in the morning just like you... you get the idea. As if it takes a genius to fathom that they are, after all, only human. But non-celebrity memior..?

What really surprised me was the discovery I made when leafing through the sleeve notes to the Strapping Young lad album 'Alien' that a friend of mine had lent me. No, the fact that I was disappointed by their appearance wasn't the surprise, and nor was the fact that I was disappointed by the music, which isn't a patch on the albums I already have, 'City' and 'Heavy as a Really Heavy Thing' – the reason for this being that the band appear to have slumped from making a wall-of-noise industrial strength racket to fairly MOR nu-metal fare, replete with wanky solos (you can't blame it all on the production). What struck me was the page of credits. A paragraph of credits for each musician. No, I didn't bother to read them all. It was the principal. Ok, so all bands have some assistance in the recording of their albums, all bands use amps and other equipment and have preferred brands of gear, all bands have friends and family and fans and managers and roadies and groupies and engineers and bands they've played with, bands they're influenced by, blah blah blah. We don't need to know about it. And thanking your mum's ok if it's your first record and you're a 15 year old kid in a wet, drippy indie band, but for hairy, hoary old rockers to do it is fucking tragic. I for one prefer to think of my hairy, hoary rock idols as having been spawned, or grown like mould on a slice of bread in the dank bowels of hell rather than having parents. And certainly not mothers they love and go round for Sunday dinner with. It's just not rock 'n' roll, man. But it seems that this is emblematic of a wider issue, regarding the way that people – individuals, artists bands, whoever – present themselves a lot more openly now, a point I've touched on previously when discussing the lack of restraint some people seem to have when sharing everything – and I mean everything – with the world and his dog via their blogs.

This also set me thinking about the way we perceive bands more generally. Specifically, it set me thinking about the way I perceive bands more generally. Of course, as one grows older, one's perception changes somewhat. Some of that has to do with a growing awareness of the process – the one whereby a band records an album puts out a single some time ahead as a taster, to create a buzz, and then another one a couple of weeks before or after the album, does a round of promotional interviews, a tour, put out another single (often using live tracks recorded on the tour to save having to record any additional b-sides and maybe to help plug the previous album) then go off and work on the next album. Rinse and repeat, every couple of years or so. Of course there are exceptions to the rule and some occasional deviations from and variations on the pattern, but that's the general framework. I'm not sure precisely when I became aware of the 'rules' – probably in my early teens, when I started collecting records properly, and buying new singles and albums in the week, or even on the day – of release. Partly out of a fear of the limited edition selling out, and partly through excitement and anticipation. And having a rather obsessive streak. But with that kind of knowledge, a certain degree of mystery is lost. Up to the dawning of that awareness, songs got into the charts, were played on the radio – I always listened to the Top 40 on Radio 1 and watched 'Top of the Pops' – and

The Changing Face of Consumerism

they'd be around for a while and you could go to Woolworths or WHS and pick them up a while later. I had no idea about *the process*.

Things are very different now, of course. Airplay starts about 2 months before a single release, it makes a stratospheric entry into the charts – or fails to chart despite being a release by a big-name band – then plummets off the radar. If you don't buy a single within a week or two of release – unless it's one of those that lingers in the charts for fucking months – you'll struggle to find it. And you'll not get it in Woolworths because they're ceasing the sale of CD singles this year. I haven't been into WHS in about a decade because they stocked nothing of interest to me once I had discovered that my tastes were less mainstream where music – and books – is concerned. Even albums, apart from the big-selling and standard titles become more difficult to find in high street stores like HMV after a not-so-long time. This only serves to accentuate just how driven by marketing formulae the industry is.

It's perhaps less of an issue with smaller bands, and bands that are on the kind of labels that simply can't operate in keeping with the commercial model. Some bands and labels are practically cottage industries. This again reflects the nature of our contemporary society, as characterised by, simultaneously, an immense homogenisation of culture as represented by the mainstream, and an extreme fragmentation, as represented by anything outside the mainstream. While the mainstream becomes increasingly centred around mass-production – which seems to run contra to the public's craving for greater access, the non-mainstream relies on a closer relationship between the artist and the fan. In order to promote their work, the band – or writer, or whoever – is required to get out there and do it themselves. But perhaps this isn't such a contradiction: the more famous (i.e. mainstream) the celebrity, the more access the public wants. And because direct interaction simply isn't feasible, it has to be made through social networking and through guts-on-display biography and memoir.

I also believe that new bands often have a certain enigma, which soon fades. The trick is to maintain a degree of mystery. But so few succeed in doing so, and it's at that point that some – much – of the magic is lost. Hearing a song for the first time, one can wonder who the band, what they look like. But television and magazine interviews can very quickly spoil things, when you learn that they're a bunch of trendies with nothing to say for themselves. And they only have the one song that's any good. You feel cheated.

So, returning to my central point, namely the accessiblisation of celebrities, there's little doubt in my mind that the Internet, and particularly networking sites such as MySpace, has had a profound effect on the trend toward this accessibility. The celebrity has a blog. The fans can read it, and can comment on it, directly, immediately. It's a lot closer in communication terms than the old fan-mail which may earn a mass-produced signed photo by way of a response. Indeed, MySpace even promote their featured 'celebrities' with the lead 'get closer to...' But is it so desirable to do so? For a start, there's nothing worse than meeting one of your heroes only to discover that they're a complete twat. It spoils everything and it's impossible to view their work in the same way ever again. And discovering a noisy rock band are a bunch of mummy's boys is just as bad. And many writers and musicians are quite shy, retiring, private types. Moreover, many writers will almost inevitably use autobiographical elements within their fiction, and that's as much as they're wanting to give away. What's so wrong with that?

I'm not suggesting that such interaction in any way encourages stalking, probably quite the contrary (after all, there's less 'need' if it's all out there). But it does indubitably alter the relationship between the artist and the fan. There's now a certain expectation for the artist – or celebrity – to put it all out there in public. But how much information do we need? I'm all for the demystification of the creative process in the way Burroughs did with the cut-ups, for example. But a little bit of mystery goes a long way. Yes, it's perhaps unhealthy to place 'celebrities' and artists (in whatever medium) on pedestals and the acceptance that they are human and fallible is important. They may be special, but they're not deities. Treating them as such isn't good for anyone. Diva syndrome's not pretty or conducive to the creative process. So, whatever the prevailing obsession with celebrity dirty laundry and lifestyle may be, sometimes, less really is more and yes, you really can have too much of a good thing.

Christopher Nosnibor

The Changing Face of Consumerism XIII: The Cost of Living: When Inflation Increases Beggars Belief

The other day I was walking through town on my way home after an arduous day's chairpounding. I had my MP3 player on (an Alba I bought in Netto several years ago, the battery door of which is sellotaped on after one of the hinged broke) and it was blowing a gale as I weaved my way through clusters of ambling clods. I was suddenly aware of a man standing to my left, stepping into my path and waving his hands as one does when trying to flag down a car in an emergency, a half-rolled cigarette in one hand. He spoke, but I couldn't hear him for my music. I stopped, removed an earphone and begged his pardon, half-expecting him to ask if I had a light.

'Got any spare change?' he asked.

'I haven't, sorry,' I replied.

'How about a pound coin?' he said, without missing a beat. He indicated the sleeping bag and three rucksacks propped against the wall of the building behind him. I'd clocked these from the off, and had taken him for a backpacker.

'I'm sorry, I haven't got any change,' I repeated. A pound coin is still change, albeit moving somewhere beyond the 'small change' category.

'Five pound note?' he pressed.

I didn't have a fiver. In fact, having only been to the bank at lunchtime, I had only a solitary twenty pound note on my person. I suppose I could have made him go through the denominations until he got to twenty, before having to admit that I did have a twenty but it wasn't spare, or asking if he had any change for it, but instead simply told him that I was sorry, but didn't have any money. I might have added that I didn't or a light for that fag he was halfway through rolling either, because I'd given up smoking some years ago after it became too expensive for me to sustain even a five a day habit, but thought better of it and went on my way.

I'll admit that more than I felt guilty for not having been able to help, I was taken aback by his brazen pushiness. Unshaven, in my scuffed Chelsea boots and second-hand jeans, did I look like I had a fiver to spare? But as I continued home, I pondered the exchange further.

The news media has made such a big deal about inflation and the sharp increase in both unemployment and the cost of living in recent months. The families of middle England are the hardest hit, apparently, the cost of fuel having rocketed, making the daily commute, the school run and the supermarket shop substantially more expensive, against a backdrop of reduced benefits for families, etc. Yeah, right. From the bottom up, we're all in trouble.

Christopher Nosnibor

The Changing Face of Consumerism XIV: Surviving the Global Economy Crisis: Why Homebrewing is the Way Forward

In the same way that I'm not really one for New Year's resolutions, I'm not one for faddish radical lifestyle changes that last a matter of weeks or months, either. So many pointless gym memberships, so many items purchased at exorbitant cost only to be abandoned and left to gather dust after the first three months, so many short-lived diets that fall by the wayside after a couple of weekends of heavy social engagements... for what? Me, I try to adopt simple, small, but sustainable lifestyle features.

As the term 'credit crunch' falls out of favour and 'recession' and 'double dip' become the terms of the now, and one cannot help but wonder if 'depression' might not be in common usage before too long, it seems appropriate to reassess more than one's finances. After all, it's not simply an approach to monetary matters that's brought us where we're at now, in the midst of a very grave financial crisis: no, it's the culture more broadly. Of course, I'm generalising when I say that everyone's out for themselves, that no-one gives a toss about anyone or anything else beyond their own self-interest, their own comfort, their own material gain, their own pleasure.

And don't get me wrong, I think pleasure's important. But in our culture of greed and self-interest, it seems that many pleasures, and many material gains are made at someone or something else's expense. Arguably, it was ever thus, and I'm not for a second about to suggest that feudalism was based on egalitarian principles that gave the serfs a great

60

deal, but it seems to me that capitalism is very much founded on the principal of the survival of the shittest, a nepotistic model in which privilege breeds privilege and those at the top are there because they've trampled all over those at the bottom to get there and continue to do so at every opportunity in order to widen the gap and maintain their own position in the upper echelons.

Unfortunately, I don't think that recent events mark the beginning of the end of capitalism, although I would like to think it's been dealt a blow that will force some very serious reappraisal. And I think the 'age of austerity' that's being touted is similarly bollocks. However, given this week's news that the average price of a loaf of bread looks set to rise by ten pence due to Russia's ban on grain export following a failed harvest, everyone is going to feel the pinch. Will the majority cut back on extravagances? Probably not, just as he banks haven't stopped handing out mega-bonuses (and following a return to profit for some of the big name banks here in the UK, boomtime bonuses look likely to be on the cards once more as the hard times following the crash are quickly forgotten. Will big businesses – or individuals, for that matter – ever learn from history?

It's a complete lack of restraint and an inability to resist temptation and greed-driven cravings that have driven not only the western, nay, global economy, but the culture of the last thirty years. Somehow I doubt that any changes that do come about as a result of this mess will be early as radical as all that though, because I really don't think you can change human nature, which is predisposed to greed and all the rest. History shows us that much, however steadfast our refusal to learn from it. And yet... and yet, I still feel the urge to try my best to educate.

Now, I know for many that home-brewing is something that has some terrible and unpleasant connotations. Recollections of their dads or certain friends presenting them with some foul-smelling murky fluid with the consistency and flavour of the silt dredged from the bottom of the river. As someone who's been brewing since I started at university, there are some for whom I will be that friend. To those, I can of course only apologise. But practice makes a lot better, if not actually perfect, and fifteen years on, I have a lot more hits than misses when it comes to beer. And wine, and cider, and mead...

But what has homebrewing got to do with the trashed economy? Well, for starters, it's cheap, while bought alcohol isn't – not even in the supermarkets, not really, despite what the media say. Ok, so some piss-weak lager might still be 60p a can, but at 2.2%ABV, the argument for increasing taxes etc., in order to curb alcohol-fuelled violence and all the rest in this basis is almost as weak as the booze. Nothing you'd actually want to drink is actually cheap. But what about the dirt-cheap white ciders favoured by tramps and street-drinkers? Yes, it cheap and very very nasty and for addicts only. Life must be bad for anyone to drink this stuff anyway: do we really want to drive these poor sods to meths?

Given that the vast majority live in urban areas, living a 'Good Life' type existence of self-sufficiency is out of reach for most of us, to suggest that it's even something to aspire to would be ridiculous. No-one has the time or the space. But anyone with a small back yard can grow tomatoes or peppers or runner beans in a tub, cut and come again lettuce in a window-box or a range of fresh herbs and even chillies on the kitchen windowsill. It doesn't take too much space – or effort, in real terms – to home-brew half-decent booze. If everyone produced something, essentially enough for personal use and perhaps a little over, it would go some way to alleviate the pressure of rising prices.

Of course, it's illegal to sell homebrew, unless you've got a licence, which essentially defeats the object anyway. But you can give it away. And swap it for stuff. I'm not suggesting a bartering revolution or bringing about the demise of capitalism. I am, however, suggesting that entering barter-based micro-economies, we could make life easier and the world a slightly better place.

Christopher Nosnibor

The Changing Face of Consumerism XV: Manic Street Preachers in Cover Controversy... or Censorship?

I was rather astonished to read that the UK's leading supermarket chains, Asda, Morrison's, Tesco's and Sainsbury's have 'banned' the new Manic Street Preachers album on account of it's 'inappropriate' artwork.

Well, ok, so further reading reveals that they haven't actually banned it (as *Kerrang* reported, and supported with a quote from bassist Nicky Wire "Supermarkets won't accept the album cover, which I am really startled at. You can have the Pussycat Dolls poledancing, but you can't have our album cover.") and aren't refusing to stock it. They're simply refusing to carry its original artwork, and will instead display the CD in a plain slipcase.

The cover of *Journal for Plague Lovers* features a painting by Jenny Saville of a boy, who may (or may not, depending on your interpretation) have a bloodied face. Whether or not I think it's a 'good' painting isn't the point. But does the fact it doesn't shock me in any way make me desensitized?

I can't help but agree with the band's bewilderment at the decision, and the point made by James Dean Bradfield: "You can have lovely shiny buttocks and guns everywhere in the supermarket on covers of magazines and CDs, but you show a piece of art and people just freak out"

While *The Guardian* ran a music blog by Jonathan Jones that contended that this 'raises the interesting possibility that hand-made, painterly images now have more power to shock than conceptual artworks' (and he may have a point), I would also say that it reinforces the depressing – rather than interesting – possibility that the world's gone mad and is riddled with hypocrisy.

To unpack this a little, the supermarkets in question aren't making any kind of judgement regarding the contents of the CD. Fair enough, it's certainly innocuous and harmless enough compared to the wall-to-wall misogyny and glorifications of violence that proliferate across many of the rap albums in the charts, but then, by the same token, if the problem with the cover is that it's thought-provoking and hints at darker aspects of life, then surely the album should be subject to the same kind of scrutiny. But that, of course, would require some actual interrogation, rather than an immediate and not very rational knee-jerk reaction that surrounds anything to do with children, the likes of which saw Chris Morris' truly brilliant *Brasseye* and Channel 4 subject to a mass of moral outrage for daring to parody a subject as grave as paedophilia. And, more saliently, I believe, to refuse to stock an album that's guaranteed to be a top 10 hit and probable number 1 on the week of release won't send a message to anyone and will simply mean that the supermarkets won't be getting a cut of the sales profits. And that would never do: the shareholders would have a fit. I daresay the record company might have something to say too. As it stands, however, the controversy is more likely than not to boost sales, for all sorts of reasons.

Ironically, the supermarkets that are, by their actions, giving the band some free promotion (there's no such thing as bad publicity, right? Just ask Jonathon Ross: a furore, a few weeks of vilification and a three-months suspension and a BAFTA at the end of it all) are the kind of corporate giants that the Manics railed against at the start of their career, back when they were full of bile and were all about political sloganeering against the system rather than being a part of it.

Are these supermarket chains guilty of uneven censorship, or simply reactionary hypersensitivity in a climate already rife with moral indignation over the most trivial of things? Either way, the end result is the same, and the latter leads to censorship however you look at it. It's a slippery slope, alright, and people need to speak up and to take action. Because if you tolerate this, your children will be next....

The Changing Face of Consumerism

The Changing Face of Consumerism XVI: Real, Real, Real

Just as the nature of consumerism has changed dramatically during the course of the last decade – not to mention the last half-century – so the nature of industry has also metamorphasised. In so-called 'developing' countries (it's a questionable term. Technological advances could be seen as development, but an exponential increase in fossil fuel consumption and an insatiable need for unsustainable resource is rather akin to 'developing' a 40-a-day smoking habit coupled with some heavy drinking), Industrialisation has caught on, dragging them into the global marketplace. By this, of course, it simply means that large corporations can circumvent domestic legislation in favour of giving workers rights and exploit an fiscally impoverished workforce even more ruthlessly. Driving costs down is good for business, as it increases profits, and the shareholders and the City love that.

As more manufacturing has been 'outsourced' to developing countries, the nature of employment in the 'developed' countries has moved toward tertiary service industries. Collar colours aside, the most fundamental difference between service and manufacturing industries is the tangibility or physicality of the product. The closest you'll get to seeing or holding your insurance or shares, for example, is in the form of a certificate or other printed document. When you think about it, these objects which represent the thing in itself but are not in actuality the thing in itself – i.e. the signifier to the signified – you're buying a concept more than an actual product. Of course, this is simply how money works: the ten-pound note in your wallet is not actual money, but a physical symbol of money. The balance in your bank, if you're fortunate enough to be in the black, does not mean there's really £500 that you own just sitting there. This is common knowledge, but it's hard to separate the concept from the reality. You do not have any real money. No-one ever sees 'the money'. Tom Cruise could yell till he's blue in the face, he's never going to be shown the actual money, just more printed paper that promises to pay the bearer a designated sum on demand. But try making that demand and all you're likely to get another sign or representation.

We live in a virtual world. In his writing on 'The Political Unconscious', Fredric Jameson theorises that one feature of postmodernity is a reality that is infinitely deferred. This theory is now the reality as we exist in our virtual worlds projecting ersatz avatar versions of ourselves into the ether. It becomes impossible to distinguish the real from reflection, not only for others, but for ourselves. Do we become the identities we project, or do they become our real-life selves when the layers of the onion that is the multi-faceted personality are peeled back one by one?

On a personal level, my real-life self and virtual self are indeed separate but given to occasional and significant crossover. And so it is that we both like music and books with a passion, but struggle to get to grips with the modern trend for downloading. It's ok: Deleuze and Guatarri convinced me I'm ok because a schizophrenic mindset is the only sane response to the postmodern, late-capitalist society I find myself in.

Stumbling around the house trying to avoid the partially organised and rather precarious stacks of CDs and books in the office and groaning each time I try to accommodate a new purchase onto the shelf or rack, I can completely understand why people would want to declutter, to reduce their lives. Yet try as I might, I find myself unable to separate the intangible – the music or the words – from the tangible, the physical – the record or CD or the book.

Nevertheless, I like my intangibles to present a physical form. The way I respond as a reader to words contained in the books I read is a complex process, which, while admittedly develop through conditioning and personal experience, is nevertheless intertwined with the act of reading. An audiobook may contain exactly the same words, but will not cause me to react in the same way. On a purely personal feel, the act of reading also entails the turning of the page, the look, feel and smell of the book. The quality of the paper, however poor, the print, the formatting, the cover, while peripheral, are all integral to varying degrees in combining to create the experience as a whole. Even the process of sourcing books is a part of the relationship I have with it: memories are made in the locating of a book in a little secondhand shop while on holiday just as much as they are of recalling where I was when I read the book, and how I was feeling at the time.

The same is true of music and many other objects – objects that now clutter my home, but collectively tell a version of the story of my life. This isn't to suggest in any way that I am my possessions, or that my possessions own me and not vice versa. Nor would I really describe myself as a materialist in the conventional sense.

Perhaps it's my age, but I want to feel as though I'm actually buying something when I part with my money. Yes, I know that in reality that it's the production – the recording, the creative process – that is where the bulk of the cost actually lies. The physical object – the CD or the book – coat pence each to manufacture. A CD may cost in the region of 49 pence to produce, but paying the artist a wage of some description, that allows them to eat while they record the album, for which it's necessary to hire (and pay for) a studio, engineer., etc., soon becomes a substantial expense, and one that must be recouped – usually before the artists gets paid, too. Then there are the designers, the PR people, and all the rest. So, the difference in production cost between a CD and an M3 version of an album comes down to the medium. However, this is only partly true: depending on the size of the manufacturing run, the cost of producing a CD is in fact negligible, and the same is true of a book. Yet as a consumer, I don't really care about these matters: it feels like the difference is a yawning chasm that spans half the universe.

It's not just the sound quality (I know the sound of MP3 files has improved enormously in the last few years, but even if an MP3 isn't compressed to fuck, it's still inferior to the digital spectrum we were once sold as being the glory of the CD, which in turn lacked the vibrance and depth of vinyl. Forget clarity, that clinical crispness strips something from the recording that can't be substituted or compensated, and the MP3 is the CD's poor cousin, lacking the physical presence and lyric booklet in much the same way that a virtually turning page is not, however hard it might pretend to be, a fair substitute for an actual page.

I'm aware of the issues of storage, perhaps more than most. 1,500 or so LPs and 12" singles, 600 7" singles and in excess of 2,000 CDs are a real bastard to house in a two-bed terraced property, and to move when it comes to relocation. But at least I know where my money's gone and what I need to insure. Picking up a storage device no bigger than an audiocassette knowing that it contains not only my entire music collection, but also music to the value of something in the region of £30,000 is almost inconceivable. The same is true of a virtual library. The fact that a fire tearing through the house would – or could – have the same effect regardless of my choice of 'file' type is really beside the point.

It's curious to note how times have changed: time was when an extensive library of books and an expansive record collection were perceived as accomplishments. They inspired respect, even awe. Now, the owners of large volumes of material possessions are considered to be simply behind the times, information dinosaurs plodding a Luddite land of clutter that's cumbersome and difficult to navigate. Why would anyone want a 10-volume encyclopaedia when mankind's entire learnings can be obtained on-line via Wikipedia (or other sites if more specialist knowledge is required, but why would you want that, really, unless you're a real nerd)? In fact, what's the point of a space-hogging PC base unit and monitor when you can have everything you need on a tablet? A music collection and library that not only occupies considerable space, but cost a fortune and took a lifetime to accumulate seems entirely redundant beside a small, flat piece of digital kit that costs around £300 and can be transported anywhere. And I suppose if you're happy or able to accept a life of precarity, instability, endless mobility, that's fine, but it's not for me.

In fact, for many, owning music seems superfluous when you can stream it all via Spotify. It frees up funds to purchasing other ephemeralities and experiences. Again, the idea of a life recorded on Facebook is one that doesn't appeal to me. The public nature of the medium aside, I struggle with the concept of a reliance on something that may disappear at any time. If there's one thing we've learned in our world of rapid development is that technology attains obsolescence at an evermore speedy rate. There was a time, believe it or not, when the 8-track, the cassette and the videotape were all cutting edge. Betamax, laserdisc and minidisc were all the future, yet despite the qualities these media offered, early adopters were left out of pocket and out of style, not to mention out of the technology loop. CD was supposed to supersede both vinyl and the audiocasette – yet strangely, the MP3 killed both CD and tape while vinyl hangs in there, with a whole new wave of audiophiles sustaining a market that previously didn't exist. I digress: the point is that Facebook could be next year's MySpace, and a life on line is only a transient representation of real life: it's a history that can not only be easily misrepresented and misappropriated, but one that could even more easily be erased. Obviously, nothing's forever, but the physical – especially if backed up, duplicated somehow – has a greater capacity to be futureproof than anything that relies purely on the intangible (but then I find the idea of playing a virtual guitar while playing at being in a virtual band equally abhorrent and not just a little strange Step away from the console, pick up a real instrument, learn to play and form a proper fucking band if you have any interest in Rock Stardom!).

I'm not doing technology down as such – at all, in fact – but can you imagine future generations, instead of looking through albums and biscuit tins of family photos and shoeboxes of postcards and correspondence, gluing themselves to a screen and reminiscing about the day that prompted that romantic email, the wonderful day out to the coast captured magnificently in 6 megapixel digital colour, or even the idea of returning to that book you so loved in college and forwarding your friend or child the Kindle download to read and share the wonder? In all of the streamlining, the decluttering, something has been lost. An on-line playlist is not a direct or equal substitute for a lovingly-compiled mix-tape with lovingly-written, hand-scribbled notes on a piece of paper torn from an exercise book and inserted, tightly-folded, into the plastic case. If, as Marshall McLuhan suggested, the medium is the message, what sort of message is a medium that's so *theoretical* say about our times and its users?

The bottom line is that if I'm spending money on something, I want something to show for it. I'm not suggesting that it needs to be big to justify the expense, but in a world where so little is fixed, stable, reliable, there's a lot to be said for keeping it real as a means of keeping it grounded, and as a way of keeping it accessible in the future.

Christopher Nosnibor

The Changing Face of Consumerism XVII: Check the Meaning* - First Direct's Advertising Gaffe

Before I open my mouth or commit words to a page (in which I also include posting those words online), I make sure – as a rule – that I know what I'm talking about. After all, no-one likes to be descended upon and criticised without mercy, and I'm no exception.

If I'm going to use a phrase, in any context, I make sure I know what it means, in case I'm saying something that conveys a meaning entirely different from the one I want to express. Sure, I do make the occasional mistake, as those who turned up to my Whisperin' and Hollerin' review of the latest Darren Hayman and the Secondary Modern single, armed with pick axes and shovels to demolish my work will confirm. Being pilloried as a 'nitwit' stung rather, although there was a real sense of achievement in my piece being described by one reader describing it as 'the worst review ever'. I digress, but the point is, even when writing my short reviews, produced in relative haste, I do make every effort to do my research and to use words and phrases correctly.

For this reason, I find the latest advert for First Direct, a division of HSBC, irritating beyond belief.

You heard the girl right. While in her job at the call centre, where she's happy and loving her work rather than wanting to murder her colleagues before slitting her own wrists, she tells her customer pleasantly and conversationally, "I'm like a fish out of water, me."

Ok, so it's supposed to be a reference to the whale habits that are a feature of the first scene, and a way of showing that First Direct is

The Changing Face of Consumerism

different, that it employs UK-based staff who are quirky, friendly and chatty, rather than characterless drones who rely on scripts as they sit in their offshore sweatshop call-centres. But that's not actually what she's saying. "A fish out of water" is not a person who's "a bit different," but a person in an alien environment, someone who's struggling, out of their depth and doesn't know what they're doing.

She follows this remark with "We're all like that here." Wow. So First Direct employ whole offices full of staff who haven't a fucking clue – and talk complete and utter bollocks to boot. It doesn't exactly instill confidence, does it? Imagine the scenario: you ring up and ask for you balance. The person at the other end of the phone tells you you're a thousand pounds in credit. Great! But what they actually mean is that you're a grand overdrawn. And so on.

It pains me that this didn't occur to whoever came up with the concept for the ad, or those who wrote the script. It similarly pains me that at no point in the process did an agency exec or anyone from First Direct's marketing department spot this. It pains me, because, despite what Darren Hayman's fans, in a lather about the supposed fact that my reviews are 'Just really badly written and without any real grasp of grammar, spelling or what the album is about,' I know that if I was in advertising, I would have spotted it. I would have pointed it out (and probably have been slammed down by my manager, who's a semi-literate cock-end but has a better haircut and more expensive suit). So what can we learn from this? Answers on a comment, please.....

* I think Richard Ashcroft is rubbish, boring and self-indulgent, but I thought the title appropriate, and in using this reference, figured it might demonstrate my point about doing my research, whether it's within my field or not.

Christopher Nosnibor

The Changing Face of Consumerism XVIII: Down on the Street

Only just a few days into January and already the sales reports from the high street are beginning to filter through for the run-up to Christmas. It's difficult to imagine that anyone will be surprised by the fact that broadly, sales have been rather poor and substantially weaker than hoped, and that as a percentage of retail sales, online transactions account for a larger proportion than ever before.

Sky News report, 'There is one factor common to the trading statements from Next and John Lewis – an increase in online sales that has propped up the overall results.'

The on-line article continues, 'In the case of Next, it's [sic] Directory service recorded a 16% increase between 2010 and 2011 for like-for-like sales. Sky News has been told that online sales account for roughly 90% of this figure. With regards to John Lewis, online sales for the five weeks to December 31, 2011, were 27.9% up on last year.'

Apart from exemplifying the kind of statistically-dense reporting that's likely to bamboozle the average reader and providing a practical demonstration in the kind of journalism that uses a proliferation of numbers in lieu of meaningful analysis, what we are supposed to extrapolate from this is that the figures speak for themselves. Of course, this is patently untrue, because the figures, bald and devoid of context are in themselves virtually meaningless. The scant analysis offered by the unnamed reporter does little to shed any real light on the implications of the figures when they ask 'What can we learn from this? Well essentially that we, as shoppers, are inherently lazy and becoming increasingly more so,' adding 'There is nothing wrong with that. If we can shop without leaving our desk or home then we are choosing to do so.' Really? There's a lot wrong with being inherently lazy, on so many levels, but of more importance here is the fact that shopping from one's desk (something many employers would surely disapprove of, and which could constitute misuse / abuse of company systems) or home does not necessarily equate to being lazy. I would contend that lethargy has nothing to do with it, and that the laziness of consumers is nothing in comparison to the laziness of the journalists proffering such poorly-considered evaluations of the 'facts'.

For starters, the article fails to take into account the fundamental fact that high-street (or out of town) shopping – real-life shopping – is hell. Never mind, as was mentioned in the BBC's TV report, that the opening hours of high-street retail outlets are both limited and limiting, and that on-line shopping affords the convenience of 24/7 open hours, which are handy for those who work sociable hours (I say this because those work work anti-social hours aren't stuck in an office or other place of work between the hours 9am and 5pm, when shops are open, and if you've ever tried to do any serious shopping within the confines of a lunch hour Monday to Friday, you'll appreciate that it's not only nigh on impossible, but more hellish than Beelzebub's oven).

Discounting the Sartrean hell that is other people momentarily, there's the fact that comparing the prices different retailers charge for the same item is considerably more straightforward and less time-consuming on-line than on foot. And of course, time is money, supposedly. Undoubtedly, that time is the most precious commodity an individual can have is part and parcel of the hectic technology-driven lifestyles that facilitate both on-line shopping and global commerce. If workers do spent time at their desks shopping on-line, it could be that they're time-wasting skivers, but could just as readily be because they're too busy to take a proper lunch break in which to hit the shops, which have probably relocated to an out-of-town shopping precinct.

According to the Sky article, 'The trick for retailers is how best to facilitate that and how they combine an online store with their high street shops whilst keeping both profitable.' No kidding. By making your presence as a business prominent via the most channels available, with particular emphasis on those where the most customers are, then you'll fare better than if you don't. The adage 'Location, Location, Location' still has merit, and applies to the virtual world too. As for keeping outlets profitable, that's surely how business works, period.

Sky's report concludes with the observation that 'Both Next and John Lewis know their customer base well and play to it with success' (fine, except according to the figures, Next's overall sales are only fractionally up, and its high street sales have dropped dramatically, a point that provided the focus of *The Guardian's* reporting of the same information, with Zoe Wood writing, 'Analysts estimated that like-for-like sales in Next stores fell more than 5% in the last two months of the year, resulting in a worse than expected 2.7% decline for the six months to 24 December. That weakness was offset by a strong performance at home shopping arm Directory, where sales jumped nearly 17%. Together the divisions delivered growth of 3.1% which was in line with guidance given to analysts in November').

The reporter ends their piece by opining that 'Retail is Darwinian, the survival of the fittest. Success and survival comes to those who change and adapt. The old adage is the true: the customer is always right.' This is blatantly untrue, and blindly propagates the myth that markets are consumer driven. As I have bemoaned variously, I feel largely uncatered for as a consumer. It's not even the obscure items, that I would expect having difficulty with, that present the biggest problems. If I want something unusual, there are niche stores – granted, usually on-line – that stock them. I'm talking about specific books, records, storage solutions, brand footwear at prices I'm willing to afford (£95 for a pair of DM Chelsea boots is obscene however you look at it) homebrewing equipment and other such items. But try finding something simple, like decent oven mitts, a ceiling-mounting light for the bathroom designed to work with a fitting that runs in conjunction with the wiring for an extractor fan, jam jars, etc., and you'll probably struggle. I can't be the only one seeking these items, and can therefore only conclude that others make do with whatever alternatives and close matches are readily available. How does this indicate a market tailored to the consumer?

Moreover, if I find myself making an increasing number of purchases on-line because I frequently return from town empty-handed, having been unable to find the specific item I was searching for, how is that an example of consumer lethargy? Again, by failing to cater for my needs, the high-street stores have failed their (potential) customers and driven them on-line. If retail is Darwinian, surely the survivors are the ones that stock the items that consumers actually want. After all, it's only possible to convince people that they want what they get and that they don't know what they want until they see it up to a point. If I need a new stylus for my turntable, it won't do to tell me that vinyl's outmoded and that I should get myself an iPod and docking station instead, and similarly, if the styli in stock aren't compatible with my turntable, I won't be buying one – or a new turntable for that matter, at least for as long as there are other stockists who carry compatible styli. It's really not that hard.

High-street shopping is tiring and laborious. Some people love it and will spend days trailing round shops trying on shoes and clothes and all the rest. Yet even those than enjoy such shopping expeditions will often make their purchases on-line, not through lethargy but because of the price. No-one with half a brain is going to buy an item in one place they can purchase for a third less elsewhere, especially when they know it's the item they want having already tried it on or out. On-line stores don't have the overheads of physical stores: fact. They don't have to pay out-front assistants, cleaners, heating, lighting, or, most significantly, rent on the floorspace. This is precisely why Amazon can undercut Waterstone's and HMV so dramatically (and why HMV, with their Channel Islands based tax-loophole savvy on-line arm can undercut its own physical stores, a retail model also known as shooting oneself in the foot). Of course people are going to go and buy their goods on line for less. It's simple economics.

Another piece of simple economics is that anything that isn't growth is considered recession, but to expect endless growth is unrealistic. Sure, the world's population may be continually expanding, but that doesn't mean they all want to buy the same products. Certain markets have limited potential for expansion, even mainstream mass markets. Therefore, to declare 'flat' sales or lower than projected growth a complete disaster seems unreasonable. Yet many companies will lay

The Changing Face of Consumerism

off large numbers of their workforce in light of such 'disappointing' results, and blame the recession while contributing to it and exacerbating the problem further.

But perhaps the biggest major omission in these reports is that people aren't spending because they simply don't have the money. There's a global financial crisis going on. The fact that the figures for Christmas 2011 correspond with those for 2008, only with the decreases in overall sales and the erring toward on-line sales more dramatic, reminds us that we're still in a slump. The words 'recession' and 'depression' still hang over financial reports like a black cloud. Look at the most recent unemployment figures: they're still on the up, not just in Britain, but in the US – and the US economy *is* the global economy.

Context counts, then, and against a backdrop of financial uncertainty, rising inflation, etc., etc., people are spending less money because they have less money. It's interesting to note that these reports appear on the same day that homelessness charity Shelter made public the findings of a survey they had recently conducted, which revealed that one in seven Britons has turned to credit such as a payday loan or unauthorised overdraft to help cover their rent or mortgage in the last year. Surely this is all the evidence required to establish the reason behind reduced spending. I'll say it again: people simply haven't got the money. But then, perhaps they never did have the money. The difference now is that neither do the banks, and so they're not lending it out. And if people can't get credit, then they can't spend the money they don't have on things they don't need. Better to spend the money they don't have on the things they do need, like accommodation. It's a slippery slope, of course, and where it ends is anyone's guess. But then, that's what economists do...

The Changing Face of Consumerism

The Changing Face of Consumerism XIX: Back Down on the Street, or Going for Bust

So a mere matter of days after my last piece on the struggling high street, I woke up this morning to more news of high street stores experiencing a drop in like-for-like sales in comparison to the same time last year, with HMV delivering particularly disappointing figures marked by sales being down 8.2% in December 2010. It is disappointing, too. Of the bigger chain music stores, I always preferred HMV (although Andy's records had the edge for a while both in terms of pricing and range). First and foremost, they carried a broader selection with less mainstream releases sitting alongside the chart material. And, while a tad pricey, their range of back-catalogue titles was far superior to Overprice / Virgin.

But rather than work to their strengths and make a virtue of their difference, HMV followed the template of its competitors and having killed off the (albeit limited) vinyl section in favour of calendars and games, continued over a lengthy period of time to reduce the music stock – to make room for more games, DVDs and gadgetry. When the music occupies the smallest portion of a music retailer's floor space, you have to ask questions. HMV's struggling is an example of how diversification can be counterproductive, and rather than appealing to a broader customer base, can serve to alienate the one already established. How can a music retailer seriously expect to compete in other markets already dominated by specialists. More often than not, gamers will head to somewhere like Game for games, just as you'd probably go to a clothes shop for clothes, a bookstore for books, an electrical store for electrical goods – unless, of course, they go to the supermarket for the whole lot. After a while, I stopped asking questions and also stopped going in, because each time I did I found myself leaving empty-handed and frustrated because they never had the title I was after in stock. I'd invariably end up purchasing my music on-line because I couldn't source it anywhere else.

I don't for a second mean to suggest that I'm responsible for HMV's declining sales (and I certainly played no part La Senza, the purveyors of slinky lingerie, being called into administration with a loss of 1,300 jobs, prompting headlines such as 'Lingerie firm goes bust' etc.), but while my musical tastes may be 'minority', there are many other minorities just like me, and collectively, they represent a substantial market.

As mentioned in passing in my previous piece, it's not just music that I have problems tracking down, and it's not always obscure items I struggle to find in shops either. As if to prove the point, only this week I decided I wanted to get a desk lamp. As my desk also happens to be the dining table and space is of a premium, I figured a desk lamp that clamps onto the shelves to the side of the table would be the best bet. But could I find one anywhere? Working out of time, my choices on a lunchtime were limited, but there is an Argos superstore and BHS Home Store (yes, British Home Stores Home Store) which specialises in goods for the, er, home, rather than home and clothing. A quarter of the store is given to a lighting department, but unless I wanted a lime-green desk-lamp with a regular base I was out of luck. That is, unless I wanted a ludicrously glitzy lamp shade with dangling glass bits all over it, which I most certainly didn't. Argos carry a much more substantial range of desk lights, from bendy to angle-poise, but the only clamping ones are LED lamps, which just don't give off enough light. I'd still need to put on the main ceiling light to see my screen, which defeats the purpose of a desk light I can angle in my corner without illuminating the whole room. Really, how hard can it be to find a simple item like a clamp-fitting desk lamp that takes a proper, regular bulb?

The answer is that it's not hard at all. Five minutes on-line and I found I was spoiled for choice. Even so, on-line shopping is no substitute for real shopping as it's often hard to get a sense of the precise dimensions or appearance of an item – you can't 'feel the quality' from a description and photo, however detailed. Thankfully, it transpired that a local independent store I pass on my way through town after work had the best selection of all. Once again, hooray for the independents!

Christopher Nosnibor

The Changing Face of Consumerism XX: Applied Economics and the Kindle Generation

Sometimes it's better just to keep your mouth shut. I know this. I may be opinionated, but there's a time and a place to express those opinions. More often than not, 9:05am in the office is neither the time nor the place. But sometimes I just can't help myself.

It was just another day at the office, same as any other. I was trying to do something productive, because despite my abhorrence of 'the system' and working for 'the man', I appreciate that I'm being paid (albeit not nearly enough) not only for my time, but to use that time fruitfully (when IT permit) and besides, I'm one of those people who prefers to actually make busy rather than feign being busy. Perhaps I'd feel differently if I felt any affinity with the goons who occupy the desks within conversationable proximity to mine, but endless drivel about 'Corro' and 'I'm a Celebrity' fills me with a compulsion to burrow myself into a small dark corner, meaning that more often than not, I'll bung a CD in the player or find an album on-line to stream, plug my phones in and create my own virtual cocoon in which to work. But sometimes I find it's impossible to shut out the babble, and equally impossible to keep my trap shut.

Such was the scenario the other day. Three or four people seated behind me had been discussing books. Books I wasn't bothered about. By which I mean, I'm not big on thrillers, and am wholly indifferent to the works of multi-million selling thriller author James Patterson. I was able to let the debate over whether or not his name was Patterson or

The Changing Face of Consumerism

Pattinson drift by, although I was pleased when one of the debaters thought to look him up on-line, and was also thus able to confirm the title of one of his books, courtesy of Amazon.

And so the subject moved to the topic of the Kindle.

"I love having my Kindle," pronounced the middle-aged woman in the centre of the conversation, who'd been recounting how she'd hooked her husband on a certain author's books by buying him one once. "But Kindle books are so expensive!"

"I know, I'd have thought they'd have been about a quid or something," replied the colleague to her left, a tubby guy with a beard and spectacles in his mid to late twenties.

It's a common complaint. If you read reader reviews of books on Amazon, there'll invariably be a number harping on about the price of the Kindle edition – especially with new publications – to the extent that some titles attract dozens of one-star reviews without a single mention of the writing, the plot, the characters or any other aspect of thee contents of the book itself. Many of the reviewers aren't even in a position to comment on the book, having posted their review in a fit of pique at the rip-off price being asked for the text with remarks like 'I refused to buy it at that price' and 'I've ordered the paperback instead, but will have to wait several days for it to arrive in the post. And I've had to pay shipping on top!'

In today's culture of immediacy and instant gratification, no-one wants to wait. And no-one wants clutter, either, hence the popularity of the Kindle. As the people behind me noted, it's possible to store several hundred books, which would otherwise require many feet of shelves, on a single, portable device. But no-one seems to think it reasonable that they should pay for this convenience: they want it now, and they want it cheap, or better still, for free. But of course, that isn't how capitalism works. Exploitation may be a significant feature of consumerism, with both consumer and producer being exploited for the benefit of the capitalists who hold the real power, but there has to be as degree of give and take, and if there's no profit to be made from a end product, there's simply no point in producing it, however useful it may be. But by the same token, the more useful or desirable a commodity, the higher its value in the marketplace. Whether that value is real or perceived is largely down to supply and demand, the market and marketing. It appears the perceived value of an e-book is comparatively low.

And so they whinged on in this fashion for a couple of minutes or so, bemoaning the fact that Kindle e-books are overpriced considering the fact there are no production costs involved.

As someone who has experience of publishing, both as an author and a publisher – albeit on a small scale – I felt qualified to wade in on this debate. Not that these individuals would have been aware of this: I tend to keep myself to myself, and not to talk about my writing or publishing activity in the workplace. Nevertheless, on this occasion, I found it impossible to let it go, and the fact my involvement in the publishing industry is on a small scale means it's something that's particularly close to my heart: it's something that's real and tangible, whereas with large-scale publishing – as with any large organisation – the realities become more abstracted as the process becomes increasingly distant. As with the music industry, Joe Public only conceives of the colossus: the multi-billion dollar international labels and the major-name chart acts. It's understandable, of course, but the big names – and the big money associated with them – only account for a fraction of the whole. The common misconception is that everyone who has a book published is coining it in, because they hear about the immense earnings of the likes of J. K. Rowling and E. L. James. The majority of people don't seem to realise that there are countless books that aren't on the bestseller list, that aren't published by Penguin or Bloomsbury. These are the people who buy one or two books a year, or possibly three when they raided a 3-for-2 offer at Waterstones or WHS or maybe their local supermarket. These are the people who, in the days before Kindle, would make sure the one, two or three books they purchased were at least 400 pages long because a 400-page book represents better value for money than a 250-page book or a 125-page novella that costs roughly the same. They're the people who read series books because they know the characters and are comfortable with them, but are reluctant to try anything else because they don't know what to expect: they might not like it. Better to play safe and go with what you know than risk disappointment *and* wasting money.

I don't actually believe that all artists (by which I mean musicians writers, film-makers, dancers, whatever) should be able to make a living from what they do, even if such a scenario was feasible. There simply isn't room for every artist, aspiring or otherwise, to achieve such widespread recognition as to sustain a living wage from their work, and there are many who simply aren't worthy or, to be blunt, good enough. But I do believe that all artists should be fairly paid for what they do, just as any other form of labour should receive reasonable recompense.

Christopher Nosnibor

If Kindle e-books really did all cost in the region of £1, you can guarantee that the ones who would see the biggest reduction in their cut of the profit (and there's scant profit to be made on anything costing a pound) would be the writers. It hardly seems fair that the person responsible for the creation of the product should be paid less because some consumers choose to purchase a different format. The end product may be different, but the input itself remains the same. Would an office worker – the likes of the individuals idling away large portions of their working days debating the ways in which they spend their disposable income and leisure time – consider it acceptable to be paid less for dealing with emails instead of printed letters? Of course not: in fact, I suspect the opposite would be true, and that they would probably consider it reasonable to expect to be paid more, because the reduced overheads associated with e-comms over conventional paper and envelope snail-mail would logically enhance company profits – why shouldn't they benefit? And this made for the starting point of my interjection into the conversation.

"The writers have still got to be paid," I began. "On a paperback, they get pence in royalties..."

Naturally, the precise amount varies between books, publishers and authors, and the range is immense, and the actual royalty will depend on whether or not the book sells at its RRP or at a discounted price. But, for simplicity's sake, it's not unreasonable to work on the basis of the author's royalty for a paperback being it's around the 8% (although anywhere between 5% and 10% would be considered 'average'), for hardback around 12%, and for e-books in the region of 20%. If a paperback retails at £7.99, you're looking at 63p per copy going

The Changing Face of Consumerism

The Changing Face of Consumerism XXI: Public Opinion, Booze Culture and Bartering

The local newspaper recently ran a front-page headline about proposals to open three new pubs in York's city centre. Two local breweries – The Leeds Brewery, formed as an offshoot of the York Brewery, and the Ossett Brewery, had submitted plans to take over vacant premises – one a former cafe, the others retail units, previously an estate agent and an army surplus store.

The objectors raised all of the concerns you'd expect them to. Predictably, there was concern about the city centre becoming a mecca for drinkers, that having such a concentration of licensed premises would send a message that York promoted the already endemic booze culture that is, we so often told, a leading problem in Britain that causes the taxpayer billions, and that the opening of these three new hostelries would encourage an even greater influx of stag and hen parties and cause violent, alcohol-fuelled crimes and other such sordid scenes to soar.

But these aren't the kind of places rowdy stag and hen parties would frequent. we're talking about traditional ale houses that would also serve traditional pub grub. The kind of places tourists – particularly those from America and Japan – flock to in their thousands in order to experience a slice of culture they simply do not have back home. As a historic city, visitors to York want to see and sample tradition. They also want refreshment.

Christopher Nosnibor

Other critics argued that it was essential that the city preserve retail premises for retail when conditions improve. Will they ever? This is also the same council that approved another out of town retail park, which objectors – not least of all local business owners – have opposed on the grounds that by taking the retail trade away from the city centre, the place is slowly dying. It's a complex argument, not least of all because the major chains and small independent stores serve different markets. Nevertheless, they can't have it both ways, by encouraging more retailers to move out of town and then complain that there is an abundance of vacant premises once occupied by retailers, especially in the middle of a lengthy economic downturn. Remember the words 'credit crunch' and 'recession'? For some reason, people seem to think things are improving just because the FTSE's up and more houses have sold in the last 6 months – never mind the huge numbers of redundancies announced by large employers like Aviva, Co-op and HSBC.

There is of course another angle to this, namely, if everyone's redundant, they'll need nice pubs to sit in and while away the hours as they drink their redundancy pay-offs and dole cheques.

The same day I read the article, I was walking home through the city's pub-packed centre when I ran into musician, poet, diarist and rambler Mark Wynn, a man who's inspiring in his complete disregard for any kind of consumer trends or capitalist-led operating models of industry. As ever, he'd been travelling the length and breadth of the city, the county and the country, playing poorly-paid gigs in pubs of the very sort the Leeds and Ossett breweries run and giving away most of his CDs for nothing or in exchange for a beer. It's something to be applauded. he'll never be rich, but in sharing his art, he never goes thirsty.

The Changing Face of Consumerism

Moreover, his approach represents the epitome of the punk ethic: he's out there doing it himself on zero budget and building a fanbase from a grass roots level. that's what I call sticking it to the man!

We exchanged pamphlets: I had the very last copy of my *Liberate Yourself!* pamphlet folded in my bag (there are now 100 copies in circulation, and having been left on trains, in pubs, inside self-help books in WHS and who knows where, their whereabouts and readership I haven't a clue) while he had a batch of a new A5 publication called *Dirty Work* containing some selected highlights of his spectacularly off the wall and very funny tour diaries and, stapled inside the back page, a PVC wallet containing his last album. Arguably, I was up on the deal, but these things always balance out over time (some weeks later, *Dirty Work 3* would see the light of day, containing more rampant ramblings and a new CD EP by Mr Mark E Wynn with additional text by Sam Forrest of Nine Back Alps and The Sorry Kisses, and myself). The important thing was, we had traded our art with one another, we'd both received something we wanted and what's more, the cash-free barter had taken place on the street. Retail outlets are just so last year.

The Changing Face of Consumerism XXII: The Lost Battle

February 2013 brought the news that clothing store Republic was set to call in the administrators. The news passed largely without comment, which in itself speaks volumes. As an aside, it's worth noting that most of the premises occupied by Republic stores were previously Virgin Megastores.

Republic followed Blockbuster and HMV and Jessops, who in turn followed the failure of a string of big names including Barratts, Peacocks, Game, Clinton Cards, Comet, Allders and JJB Sports the previous year and the demise in 2009 of the once-great Woolworths chain. Add to the list Mothercare, Thomas Cook, La Senza, Blacks Leisure, Past Times amongst others and the scale of the high street's decline begins to really take shape. Website retailresearch.org contains a comprehensive list of failed chains by year, and when you take into account the independent stores that have fallen by the wayside, *The Guardian*'s report in January 2013 that one in nine high street shops now stand empty hardly seems surprising. Most commentators believe we're far from seeing the last big name brands go. And yet, when Borders and Woolworths went, it sent shock waves far and wide: these were major talking points.

So what changed? Well, for starters, the sheer number of retailers going to the wall has become so enormous, with collapses so frequent that it's become increasingly difficult to keep up with them all and besides, it's not really news any more. And when news ceases to shock, people rapidly lose interest.

The Changing Face of Consumerism

Ironically when people lose interest they also forget. The so-called endowment 'scandal' isn't nearly as unexpected in context: throughout the 70s and 80s, interest was sky-high and had been even before then (November 1979 saw interest peak at 17% and inflation was also comparable in relative terms during these years). It therefore seemed reasonable to assume interest and growth would be sustained around these levels, and, if those assumptions were born out, 25 years further down the line people could expect their comparatively small investments to produce bountiful yields that would pay off a mortgage loan with change left for a new car and / or a cruise. we're simply not in the same place now.

I had considered listing all of the retailers that had gone into administration in the last three years or so, but soon decided it would make for an extremely dull read in real terms, and was an extreme length to go to in order to make a fairly basic point. Moreover, while much of what I've written while exploring the changing face of consumerism has focused on the high street, it's important to be aware that consumerism extends far beyond the domain of the shopping centre and its counterforce, the virtual shopping centre. My frequent recourse to issues concerning books and music are purely based on my persona experience as a means of using the microcosm to represent the macrocosm. In short, what I'm trying to convey is that first and foremost, everything's fucked, and second that things are changing, and at a rapid pace. When I began the first 'Changing Face' blog posts, it was impossible to predict how things would pan out – how rapid and long the downward spiral would be. And still the decline continues. we're not just talking about a few shops closing, or even banks going down, we're talking about countries going bankrupt.

Yet even then, for many, life goes on and all the economic turmoil is just 'boring news' and an inconvenience that niggles at the edge of their day to day life. Sure, the price of things is going up and wages aren't, but they still keep on spending, because, well, they do. there's stuff out there, and it needs to be bought. If you want to get ahead, forget the hat and make sure you've got the latest iPhone instead.

In such times of austerity, you would be forgiven for expecting every street in every nation to resemble Russia during the Great Depression, with people in worn, threadbare trenchcoats queueing round the block for a loaf of bread that costs a week's wages. But that simply isn't the scene that's to be seen anywhere. People are still splashing on designer duds, sharp haircuts, expensive digital kit from smart phones to tablets to cable TV and overseas holidays and, well, where does it end? People are still buying alcohol – more than ever, apparently – despite escalating prices, and people still smoke despite the fact cigarettes in supermarkets are now stored in lead-lined vaults and the price of a packet of 20 equates to half a day's work at minimum wage.

Yet the media report that people 'aren't spending' and that there's no money circulating, which is why the high street is so depressed, and the housing market is pretty much static and, well, yes, everything's fucked. But while they're clearly spending less, such broad comments are clearly misleading. Certain demographics aren't spending, and equally importantly, they aren't spending in the same way they used to. And really, this perhaps reflects the most significant point of all regarding the changing face of consumerism. The nature of commodity is changing. Just as we made a very definite shift from manufacturing to service industries through the 80s, from the production of tangibles to intangibles, so the population is more concerned with consuming intangibles over tangibles in the digital age. The high street and other businesses that deal in concrete objects are failing because no-one wants objects any more, and certainly not in quantity.

Yes, much of consumerist culture is geared toward making a statement, and if anything, the use of status symbols is every bit as prevalent and disgusting in its ostentation as it was in the 80s when yuppies briefly ruled the world. But now, less has come to be perceived as more, broadly speaking. Fewer objects, but all of a 'high end' specification is the mark of cool. Granted, smart phones have got bigger and most models of iPod are significantly bigger than the pen-drive MP3 players that were commonplace a decade ago, but it's all about the style, not to mention the functionality. With a larger capacity iPod, you can carry more music than John Pee had in his collection on a piece of kit the size of a fag packet, and a larger smart phone means you no longer need to lug a laptop around. You don't even need a 'portable' DVD player, because with streaming movies and everything stored in 'the cloud'. You don't need DVDs or a hard drive. Your entire movie library can run to a million films and you still don't require any storage space. There's no need to find a coffee shop or pub to install yourself in order to check emails or work. Your office, your media library, hell, your life, can be slipped into your pocket on your way out of the house.

But the ultimate commodity isn't space, despite what the vogue for minimalism may suggest. No, the ultimate commodity is time. All of these space-saving devices are ultimately time-savers. No-one has the time to turn a record, change a CD, turn the paces of a book (or dilly-dally choosing a book for the bus from a bookcase they haven't the time to organise or dust) and frankly, no-one has time to wait for physical media to be delivered in the mail. Digital media, from MP3 to ebooks and email is instant, and even that isn't always fast enough.

The paradox is that all of these devices, and all of the technology that was supposed to give us more time has in fact had the opposite result, because there's now even less escape from the workplace now hat the workplace can be in your pocket, and because even in our leisure time we don't switch off and are constantly checking our phones for emails, Tweets, Facebook updates,etc., etc. The leisure time we were promised has become a myth. It would be easy to blame the technology, but technology is inanimate and can bear no responsibility: it's how it's used that counts. Without getting sidetracked in a discussion of how potentially brilliant and positive discoveries have been used to destructive and / or facile ends and how this reflects the miscreant nature of man, I think that right here, right now, it's more important to consider the idea that apart from those directly affected by the closure of any given business, no-one could care less. But then, no-one could care less about the majority of current affairs, because they have no direct impact.

The global village is still considered a world away from each individual's own back door: why worry about the economic turmoil in Greece when it doesn't have nearly the same personal impact as the 'bedroom tax'? But there are other things to consider, far too many distractions: there's Facebook and Twitter and *TOWIE* and *Eastenders*.

The Changing Face of Consumerism

there's endless media demanding attention 24-7 why would anyone opt for the depressing news media when there's 24-7 celebrity gossip to be streamed? And if the people are preoccupied and passive, they'll accept anything – or simply fail to notice, or otherwise forget when the next exciting plot twist hits Albert Square. The battle for consumers who care is surely one that was lost a long time ago.

Christopher Nosnibor

The Changing Face of Consumerism XXIII: The History of the Future / The Future of History

It was while listening to Stewart Home deliver a two-hour lecture on Mail Art in the Autumn of 2011 that I found myself – not for the first time – contemplating the nature of 'the archive'. As Home passed around various bits and pieces that he himself had received through the letterbox, he spoke about Pete Horobin's decade-long DATA project, which is fascinating in itself:

> DATA – Daily Action Time Archive – began precisely on 01.01.1980 and concluded just as precisely on 31.12.1989. DATA was intended to be an extremely detailed self-portrait of an ordinary working-class artist living within a very particular moment in time within a British welfare state culture. Horobin gave everything that he produced and amassed, equal status, which is to say that complex artworks were equal to little pieces of ephemera – everything was data.

Not that Horobin is an easy man to pin down, having previously worked under various other names and with a record of changing his identity with each phase of his creative life. As such, the *Retro Dundee* blog proves to be most informative::

> The creative life of Pete Horobin terminated with the precise conclusion of DATA and the activities of the DATA Attic – as an

The Changing Face of Consumerism

open space for artists to visit and correspond – closed down. The Attic continued to be a repository for Horobin's output, and over the course of the following 15 years was occupied by various sympathetic art students.

As the Artpool website records – impermenantly – 'The concept and intent of DATA was to archive everything that related to the process of living and creating from ephemera to his photo documentation of art actions and daily rituals, such as cutting nails and shaving, to the mail art that arrived through the letterbox each day. Nothing was discarded and everything was given equal status, that is to say, a piece of ephemera was as important as a finished artwork.'

Enough context and back to the recent past, and, in particular, the way Home spoke of how the Artpool in Budapest had created a Mail Art archive. He commented on the fact that the archive had taken certain items from Horobin's project but not others, curiously rejecting actual letters and correspondence – in short, the core elements of the artist's Mail Art output. Horobin's work from his DATA project is scattered across various locations – not only the Artpool but also an array of public and private holdings across Scotland, as the post dated 1st October 2011 on the *Retro Dundee* blog attests:

Since the end of 2010 The Attic Archive has ceased to exist. Its many varied parts are now relocated in numerous museums and collections as follows –
The Museum of Childhood, Edinburgh.
The Museum of Communications, Burntisland, Fife.
Kirkcaldy Museum & Art

Gallery, Fife.

McManus Museum & Art Gallery, Dundee.

Central Library, Dundee.

Dundee University Archives.

Artpool, Budapest.

The Scottish National Gallery of Modern Art, Edinburgh.

The National Library of Scotland, Edinburgh.

The National Irish Visual Art Library, Dublin.

I wish I'd known this the last time I visited the Museum of Childhood in Edinburgh, while on a long weekend stay in the Old Town, just off the Royal Mile where the rather quirky museum is situated. But I digress. Horobin's very objective was to create an archive – the title of his project strongly alludes to the fact, while naming of The Attic Archive renders this explicit. As with any archive, the cataloguing of its contents is integral to its very existence.

How the artist will be remembered will ultimately become distorted over time, and those encountering his work through the archive will have a radically different perspective in comparison to those who came to it by other means. Of course, the idea of the archive where Mail Art is concerned is a curious one: given the nature of Mail Art, with disparate and broad dissemination being an elementary characteristic, the idea of a fully comprehensive, exhaustive archive is unfeasible. Yet perhaps now is the time there really needs to be such a thing. After all, Mail Art has essentially been consigned to history because it has been overtaken by technology.

The Changing Face of Consumerism

While there have been pockets of Mail Art revivalism, engineered through social networking sites such as Facebook in recent years, and similarly while there will no doubt have always been some form on continuance of small Mail Art networks, it's more or less fair to say that Mail Art is historical, and has been consigned to history in no small part by the ubiquitous dominance of the Internet since the tail-end of the twentieth century: Mail Art will never have the same kind of network or following again, and nor can any renaissance truly recapture the spirit of the old networks, because such activity will be born out of an attempt to recreate the past, rather than necessity.

***

In art and literature, and indeed in our conception of history, the letter has been integral. The correspondence of a great many authors has been subject to the scrutiny of scholars, and has provided a feast of material for fans, too, with the letters of countless authors being considered worthy of publication, ranging from Ted Hughes to William S. Burroughs. Indeed, Burroughs not only constructed one book – *The Yage Letters* – from his correspondence with Allen Ginsberg, but also wrote in a letter that appears in the first volume of his letters, *1945-1954*, that 'perhaps the real novel is in these letters'. The recipient again was Ginsberg, and the novel in question was *Naked Lunch*. Moreover, while Burroughs' fiction drew heavily on his own biography, much of his biography is recorded rather more accurately in his correspondence, and furthermore, given that he was a man who was notoriously difficult to get to know (like so many writers), his letters provide an insight into his character and his mind that the reflections and recollections of others do not. This is important, because for many, Burroughs' biography is of greater interest than his actual literary work.

A substantial amount of invaluable detail regarding a writer's or artist's development can also be derived from examining their personal archives, the likes of which can be found in library collections and are usually donated for the very purpose of providing resource for interested scholars. Much has been made of the different revisions and palimpsests of a number of authors from James Joyce to William Shakespeare, with the different folio editions of Shakespeare's work also providing the source of endless controversy, not least of all concerning the sequencing of his enigmatic sonnet sequence. As such, the archive – and the quality and completeness of its contents is of considerable value.

Sidestepping the questions of *oeuvre* and archive posited by Foucault in his essay 'What is an Author?' and operating on the premise that an artist's complete output can be taken as just that – anything left behind, from which slightest fragment of ephemera meaning can be wrung that helps to provide a more complete picture and thus comprehend not the unified being behind the work, but the fragmented, contradictory, multi-faceted individual. Take for example LS Lowry's rather licentious artworks discovered posthumously by way of an example. While the excavation of truckloads of previously unseen works by Picasso inevitably brings joy to the art world and provides further evidence – if further evidence was required – of his prodigious work-rate, Lowry's late sketches proved problematic for some in that they seriously challenged the established romantic image of the quiet, reclusive artist. If this proves anything, it's that the establishment – and examination – of a complete archive can provide a fascinating insight into the workings of an artist. It is only through the preservation of items and artefacts not made available to the public during the artist's lifetime, or even necessarily made for public consumption that new information, new perspectives, new readings, even new texts become available and enable those interested in doing so to get closer to 'the author'.

It perhaps goes without saying that there are issues of privacy involved here. Is it right that an artist as private as Lowry should have his personal belongings not only rifled through but publicly exhibited – something he clearly had not intended for his sketches – without the creator's permission? Perhaps not, but in death, it's no longer their decision to make, and it's often, I would assume, a difficult judgement to call for the subsequent owner of the estate. That said, how many writers or artists relent to the pressure to make their juvenilia, scrapbooks, letters and works in progress public? What may on one hand appear to be a last-gasp cash-in and a succumbing to a prurient interest in dirty laundry on the public's part could equally on the other signify the arrival of a recognition a lifetime in the waiting, and as such serves as a justification of a life of artistic struggle. So few actually achieve the recognition they deserve in their own lifetimes that surely it would be wrong to begrudge those who are celebrated in life their moment of vindication.

This clearly doesn't apply to all: some achieve immense success and fame while still alive, and similarly, many lead lives that inspire little biographical interest (or deserve to), and bodies of work that are more than adequate in themselves. Some authors really do have only one book in them, and some bands only one album. In such instances, we really do not need to dredge through their notebooks, their bedroom recordings, their less than auspicious school report and recordings of appearances in the school nativity play. Then there are the so-called 'celebrities' whose lives provide countless column inches for the scum-dredging tabloid press, despite their daily comings and goings being entirely unremarkable. What point in the biography of a twenty-one year old football player? I mean, what have they done that's worth reading about? Ultimately, the context is all.

To this end, where appropriate, at least, there is significantly more – and more value – to the establishment of a rigorously-maintained archive than mere scholastic curiosity, however. History may be a construct, but it's a necessary one, and the way it's constructed is through the piecing together of numerous archives. Similarly, just as the devil may be in the details, so the real history of culture lies not in the mainstream and the everyday, but in the small events that take place off the radar but send ripples outwards in ever-expanding concentric rings until they hit the shores a tsunami. By this time, however, distortion and refraction has occurred, and the source of the impact has become obscure. So it is with the underground press and zine culture, largely ignored by critics and academics and equally by the mainstream. Too obscure, not suitably academic, the counterculture beyond punk which has been subject to endless revision through manipulated historification and misrepresentation has been almost written out of history. Yet the preservation of these fragile documents, printed cheaply and in extremely small quantities is something that should be considered vital: so many have been destroyed or otherwise deteriorated beyond readability, yet they contain so much pertaining to the real history of literature, of music.

But what has the Internet done to 'the archive'? In some – many – cases, the digitization of existing archives has rendered them more accessible. Arguably, this is as much a curse as it is a blessing: after all, if we maintain the perspective that a writer's *oeuvre* should be viewed from a holistic perspective, and that where a writer is concerned, if they write it, it's there for consideration, and the Internet promotes a more egalitarian approach to output, blogs and on-line publications carrying the same kind of weight (and potentially achieving a much larger readership) than, say, a magazine article. Then there's the immediacy of digital publication and the fact a writer can knock out a story or piece of commentary between major works without the hassle of going through conventional channels, regardless of whether or not they have a publishing contract. It's also far easier to maintain one's profile by blogging and other forms of on-line publishing, not to mention the benefits of engaging directly with one's readership or fanbase. All of these instantaneous and instantly accessible digital works can be excellent for research, rendering the scholar's job much less laborious.

For many writers, however, letters – unless written in the line of business, i.e. exchanges with agents, editors, publishers, etc. (and how interesting or useful do such documents tend to be when trying to unravel the biographical links to a text?) – are personal in nature, and while potentially revealing and fascinating to the obsessive, were likely created for anything but public consumption.

The state of the archive is therefore in a state of flux, although at least the survival of the archive that exists already is essentially assured.

But what of the archive of the future? And what is the connection between the archive and consumerism?

The existence of the archive and how we consume our literature, art and music are intrinsically interconnected, and the technology that is part and parcel of the way we consume those commodities is also the technology that is central to its production. Digital recording means there are no master tapes. Word-processing means there are no hand-written drafts, complete with erasures and corrections. Email and social networking means there are no letters or postcards.

Scattering the archive, in the way Pete Horobin's work has been cast far and wide – is to shatter its original sense of place, its context and continuity. Yet this is precisely how we now consume everything – in fragmentary form. This isn't simply a case of postmodern theory demonstrable through practice. The problem with this type of fragmentation is that any sense of history, of context, is lost. And without any sense of linear history or context, all we have is a disparate collection of random, meaningless junk.

The way 'Reality TV' works essentially removes any overt narrative – especially commentary – from the scenarios that play out, an while many denigrate shows like *Big Brother* for being trashy and crap and full of irritating wannabes – all of which are fair and just criticisms that encapsulate much of what is wrong with such lowest-common-denominator populist entertainment, my biggest personal gripe is that they *make no sense*. It's by no means the case that I demand a solid plot and guidance from an omnipotent authorial voice to help me navigate, but when a succession of scenes of people exchanging inarticulate mumblings containing barely a complete sentence about nothing in

The Changing Face of Consumerism

particular is edited and cross-cut in such a way that any concept of linearity, time, cause or effect is buried beneath a whirl of rapid cuts, it becomes extremely difficult to understand what the fuck they're all bleating on about or why.

Irrespective of whether or not this is simply an example of my feeling the yawning chasm of a widening generation gap, the fact remain that I can discern a clear shift in the presentation of televisual media. As such, it's not just about shopping: consumerism exists on countless levels, and on every single last one of them, it's changing, and fast. The way we consume our media is changing, as is the nature of the media we consume. Text not takes second pace to images: we live in a highly stimulated visual culture – yet most commonly we consume those visuals on the tiny screen of mobile telephones. Some may call it progress, and while I'd question that, and would certainly question the benefits of that progress both now and in the long term. But if there's one thing I've shown is that there's no point in trying to halt the inexorable pace of change. The next question isn't 'how do we stop it?' because we can't, but 'what happen next?' and more importantly 'are we prepared for it?'

.